AF722968

THE COMPUTER IN COURT

K
87
K44

The Computer in Court

A Guide to Computer Evidence for Lawyers and Computing Professionals

ALISTAIR KELMAN
RICHARD SIZER

LAW LIBRARY
GOLDEN GATE UNIVERSITY

Gower

© Alistair Kelman and Richard Sizer, 1982

All rights reserved. No part of this publication may be reproduced, stored in a retrieval system, or transmitted in any form or by any means, electronic, mechanical, photocopying recording or otherwise, without the prior permission of Gower Publishing Company Limited.

Published by
Gower Publishing Company Limited
Gower House, Croft Road, Aldershot,
Hampshire GU11 3HR, England

British Library Cataloguing in Publication Data

Kelman, Alistair
The computer in court.
1. Evidence (Law) — England
2. Electronic digital computers
I. Title II. Sizer, Richard
344.207′6 KD7499

ISBN 0 566 03419 0

Printed and bound in Great Britain by
Biddles Ltd, Guildford and King's Lynn

Contents

Foreword

We are living through a revolution in the way information is handled. This is the inevitable consequence of the advances in microelectronic technology and it is certain that our methods of capturing, storing, retrieving and receiving information will be completely changed before the end of the century. The effect of the use of computers cannot be left undebated and the need for constructive criticism of the interface between the computer industry and the judicial system is apparent and essential for our system of justice to continue to work.

This book sits astride the interface and is the first stage in that debate. It explains the technology and its faults in as simple a manner as is practically possible. It explains the law of evidence in a similar way. It combines the two in an entertaining form by use of an imaginary court case. But its lighthearted approach should not be considered an indication of a lack of seriousness. For the book uses courtroom drama only to illustrate and illuminate very real problems that beset lawyers and computer professionals alike. Soon, because of the growth in the use of microcomputers and word processors, almost every document which comes before the courts will have been produced by a computer. Already lawyers need to know how to cross-examine computer personnel, what questions to ask to find latent errors in a computer's output. Computer professionals running computer installations need to appreciate the kind of cross-examination they may encounter when placing printouts in evidence. Computer professionals, such as myself, who find themselves called to give expert evidence in the courts need a limited understanding of the law of evidence and procedure. This book provides us all with the introductions we need.

I commend it as essential reading to lawyers and computer professionals alike. Its suggested method of proving that computer evidence is reliable is of particular importance. The gaps it indicates in the law caused by out-of-date statutes should be noted and filled at the earliest opportunity by Parliament. Above all the book is a filip to professional standards in the computer industry, something which I can fully endorse.

Douglas A. Eyeions
Director General
Computing Services Association

CHAPTER ONE
Faces of Computing

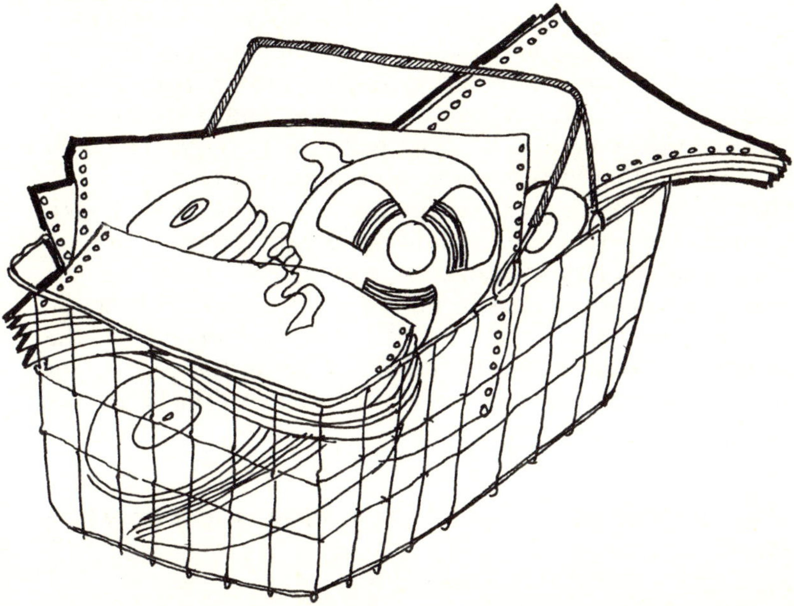

Computers can perform complex tasks, play games, draw pictures, solve incredibly difficult mathematical problems, and print the written word by the metre extremely quickly. They are now commonplace; some are expensive, many are cheap and a part of everyday life. A computer must be told how to perform any task. The instruction is carried out by a 'program' often called the 'software'. Understanding the difference between hardware (the boxes and the electronics therein) and software is important and germane to the purpose of this book. Some explanation of terms is given in Appendix A which also explains how the hardware and software interact with each other. The computer is inherently a moronically simple device in that it can only recognise one of two states such as yes or no, on or off. We show later how this works in practice. Accurate and reliable most of the time, computers can be wrong.

At one time to communicate with a computer was difficult; obscure 'languages' had to be learnt. However, great strides have been made in simplifying means of communication. Languages approximating to English and other means, are now available to, and within the understanding of, most people.

Before dealing with the book's theme of evidence and computers it is of interest to examine in what ways computers have invaded the social structure. We do this by illuminating a number of different faces of computing: pedantic, provocative, Orwellian, factual, protective, logical, proliferative and skid-row.

Working with computers tends to make one pedantic, no doubt due to the fact that everything is seen in precise terms — black or white, yes or no, on or off (the authors are no exceptions). This can lead to problems of relationships between the computer specialist and the non-specialist even though the latter may be someone who dearly wishes to be a user of a computer. So we have the first face — the pedantic face — typified by the acknowledged inventor of the computer, Charles Babbage, in his note to Lord Tennyson after the latter's poem 'The Vision of Sin' was published. The note read:

> Sir,
> In your otherwise beautiful poem there is a verse which reads
>
> Every moment dies a man
> Every moment one is born.
>
> It must be manifest that if this were true, the population of the world would be at a standstill. In truth the rate of birth is slightly in excess of that of death. I would suggest that in the next edition of your poem you have it read
>
> Every moment dies a man.
> Every moment $1\frac{1}{16}$ is born.
>
> Strictly speaking this is not correct, the actual figure is so long that I cannot get it into a line, but I believe the figure $1\frac{1}{16}$ will be sufficiently accurate for poetry.
>
> I am, Sir, Yours etc. . . .

The provocative face of computing is illuminated by the words of Jean-Paul Parrot of the Canadian Union of Postal Workers delivered to the delegates of a computer conference in 1977:

> 'Computer systems are designed largely to increase the profits of corporations and reduce the numbers of workers. Computerisation may do wonders for the profit margins of

the banks and trust companies, and it may greatly assist airline companies to inform businessmen in knowing their reservations, but this "information" does not provide workers with houses they can afford, food and clothing for their children, or safe and healthy places to work.'

The Orwellian face is illuminated by the news item concerning an alleged leakage of computer data from 4,000 US data centres concerned with medical data. Dr Gabrielli, head of a group specialising in the computerisation of medical records said:

'Computers have as much potential for good or ill as atomic energy. Unless privacy problems in handling computerised medical records are solved at once, 1984 is here already. We believe computers represent a tremendous threat to the basic human right to keep medical information private.'

The factual face is illuminated by a column in the New York Times when the initial results of the 'first-ever comprehensive computerised survey of data' was published on persons arrested in connection with the city-wide looting during the New York blackout of 1977.

Contrary to the widely publicised media analyses made immediately after the events, the computer analysis which appeared some weeks later presented a series of facts which overturned sociological theories, showing instead that many of those arrested were far from 'hopeless', having 'stronger community ties' and 'somewhat higher incomes' than those normally arrested in New York City. Specifically, thc computer statistics showed that looting suspects had a rate of 45 per cent employment, 14·4 per cent high school and college enrolment, 10·4 per cent on welfare and 30·2 percent unemployed, but not on welfare. This compared with 30 per cent employment, 12·6 per cent high school and college enrolement, 15·7 per cent on welfare and 41·6 per cent unemployed, but not on welfare, in the general defendant population.

The protective face is illuminated by a column in the Guardian which stated:

'A man, convicted three times for indecent attacks on young girls, was allowed to become an "official uncle" to a ten-year-old girl in care whom he then assaulted. The judge asked what checks had been made and prosecuting counsel said a much wider check would have been made today because the information is now available on a regional basis. And very shortly there will be a national computer which will make available details of any conviction in any part of the British Isles.'

The logical face is illustrated by the case of the Dallas construction worker who was moving to a new construction job in Chicago. Two days before he was due to leave Dallas, his new contract was cancelled because he had failed to comply with Clause R-3 concerned with maternity — his record said he was pregnant. He called Chicago and claimed that there was a mistake — he was a man and could not be pregnant. Chicago were not impressed by the claim and refused to alter their record because the industrial health clinic which had performed the physical check-up had given a positive R-3 rating. The man called the clinic who checked the computer record and confirmed pregnancy.

The following three weeks can be glossed over; the solution is the main interest. The man eventually started work in Chicago but with an amended clause forbidding maternity benefit for the otherwise statutory period.

The proliferative face is illuminated by the cartoon which showed a young boy at a desk attempting his homework. The desk was piled high with pocket computers. By the boy's side sat an anxious mother saying 'Now we must get this right — if you take 12 computers away from 20 computers how many are left?'

Computers, alas, have a 'skid-row' face as illustrated by the following scene witnessed by one of the authors. On the outskirts of Gandia, a small town in the province of Valencia, Spain, a typical Spanish market was in progress. In the hot sun, sitting along the edges of the paseo was a line of vendors — gypsies selling wild garlic, others offering live snails, yet others with oranges, chickens, rabbits, water melons and so on. Between the garlic vendors and the live-chicken vendor a man had spread a colourful rug on part of which he sat. Piled on the rest of the rug was a collection of pocket calculators and personal computers. A piece of cardboard had scrawled on it '250 pts', but there seemed little prospect of a sale. Every other vendor and shopper in sight had one of their own.

This book is about evidence from computers. It owes its existence to the effect that the decision by the Court of Criminal Appeal — that a computer-generated listing was not admissible as evidence — had on one of the authors who saw it as a potential threat to the judicial process.

The decision in January 1980 has since been reported in both the Criminal Law Review and in the official case reports. It is described later but we record here that it raises important, possible fundamental issues. These arise from the rapid growth of the computer industry with its almost impenetrable jargon and its associated specialist personnel (systems analysts, programmers, hardware engineers, operators) who have produced a problem that must be solved if trial by judge and jury is to remain respected as due process of law.

Lawyers can have difficulty in cross-examining computer industry personnel or highlighting hidden errors in computer outputs because they do not know what questions to ask. Yet the British legal system is founded on the basis of two lawyers asking questions and then arguing against each other in front of a judge and jury whose job it is to decide between the arguments. Today because of this lack of technical knowledge by many members of the legal profession certain events concerning the computer industry could be outside the law. This book tries to rectify this state of affairs. Lawyers can learn very quickly and we have presented our view of the law in a form that is familiar to both lawyers and laymen — an imaginary court case. Evidence is a huge subject and criminal and civil procedure can best be appreciated by considering examples.

In 1981 the authors produced a report,[(1)] which amongst other things, exposed the fallacy in the argument that it would always be possible for a lawyer to call an expert to testify as to the state of computer output, and that the state of accuracy would always be self-evident.

The report deals also with arguments for and against the need to modernise legislation and in fact contained a conclusion and recommendation that on balance there is probably a case for such amendment. The report stimulated debate as opinions differed, and still do, as to whether for example Section 1 of the

Criminal Evidence Act of 1965 should be extended to include computer records other than those from a trade or business. We believe that an opinion needs to be formed as to whether 'software' (the computer programs in all their forms) should be mentioned specifically. In the Civil Evidence Act 1968 the computer is defined only in terms of hardware — not a tenable definition as we attempt to show in this book.

Of particular importance, and the *raison d'être* in writing the book, is our belief that the computing and legal professions should jointly develop educational guidance and appropriate codes of practice. As a step towards these goals, the book has been written to assist members of the legal profession in correct examination of computer evidence, and to help computer professionals understand the needs of the courts, to anticipate likely courses of events and adapt their own professional activities accordingly. They could, after all, find themselves in the same position as our character, Professor Chocolate-Chip.

In our third chapter we give a brief outline of the law of evidence. Before leaving generalities we thought it appropriate to comment now on the procedures relating to criminal and civil cases so far as evidence is concerned. Non-members of the legal profession will find the comment useful background for the next chapter and for our court case described in chapters 4 to 7.

At the start of each Law Year the judges file into the Royal Courts of Justice, bewigged and gowned in a procession, following a tradition that is centuries old. Every day they administer justice according to law, following the strict rules of evidence, requiring statements to be proved by time-honoured processes, giving weight to each piece of conflicting evidence, determining questions of law and directing juries.

In a criminal case, before a prosecutor can begin to persuade a jury he must surmount the legal problems associated with the admissibility of evidence. A good defence counsel will take a number of procedural points while the jury is out of court to win the trial for his client at this stage. If he manages by any means to stop the prosecution adducing any evidence against his client, the judge has no alternative but to acquit the accused on the grounds of there being no case to answer. However, once evidence is held to be admissible the jury is recalled and it is put before them. The prosecution have to prove their case beyond reasonable doubt and defence counsel attack this construction of the evidence, suggesting instead that the evidence is both unreliable and insufficient to support a conviction.

In civil cases, generally speaking, there is no jury and the judge decides questions of fact and law alone.

Reference:

(1) *Computer Generated Output as Admissible Evidence*. BCS 'Monographs in Informatics' Series, Heyden and Sons, 1982.

CHAPTER TWO
Examples of Computer Errors

Errors in computer output can arise from a number of sources. The hardware or software may be faulty or may develop faults when interacting with other components in a particular computer network; the hardware may develop faults because it is working in an unsuitable environment (e.g. faulty air-conditioning); the software may be inadequately tested and contain hidden errors; faults may be produced by telecommunication lines used for transmission of data between computers in a network, and users may be inadequately trained. Most computer systems have safeguards that prevent undetectable 'corruption' of output. It is, however, possible for errors of a particular kind to bypass these safeguards.

In the course of manufacturing, rigorous quality and testing procedures are employed by most manufacturers. Nonetheless hardware can fail in service, often through external causes such as sudden high voltages or extreme heat. In America in the summer of 1980, the failure of a microprocessor within a large computer made by a reputable manufacturer resulted in two nuclear alerts. It was a computer operator who eventually spotted the machine error and overrode its instructions.

Software can be divided into application software and operation system software. The application software communicates with the computer through its operating system software and trains the computer for a specific task. It is useful to consider a computer system as a multi-layer sandwich as shown in the following diagram. At the top is the data, either input or stored. The data is controlled by the application software and fed into the operating system software which converts it into the series of ones and noughts (binary notation) already described, which can be manipulated by the computer. The computer sends back its response, which is converted by the operating system software into a form understood by the application software, which then controls the formation of output data for the user. (See Appendix A for an explanation of the terms mentioned in this chapter.)

Both the application software and the operating system software can contain errors in themselves but errors can also be created by the way they interact with each other and the hardware. The operating system software is closely associated with the make of computer and the way that brand of computer

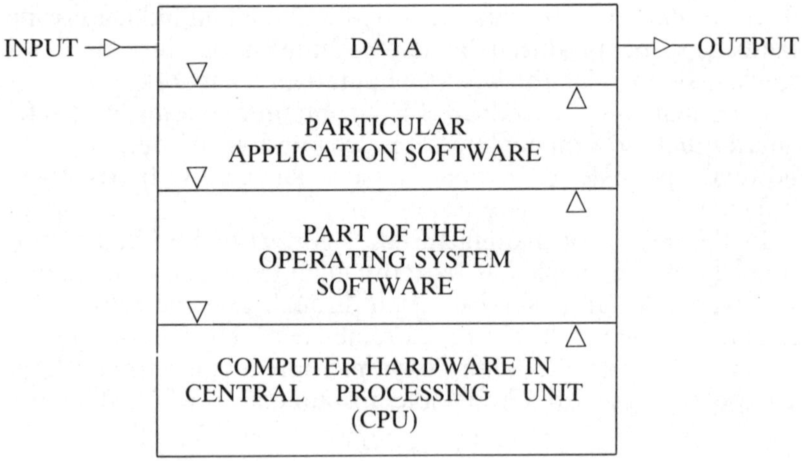

performs its operations. The application software can frequently be used on different makes of computer provided it works through a specific operating system's software. Off-the-shelf microcomputers used to be supplied with very little operating system software and often no application software. The user bought 'packages' of software to make his system more versatile and train it for specific tasks. This was like putting extra layers in the sandwich in the diagram. The rate of progress is such that operating systems and packages for micros are now available cheaply and in vast quantities from outlets (shops in the High Street) unheard of only a few years ago.

In the case of a large computer the operating system will usually be produced by the computer manufacturer. The purpose of the operating system is to control all jobs submitted to the computer, file handling, and messages passing between the computer and its peripherals, maintain a record of the processor and terminal time used by each user for accounting purposes; keep a record (log) of errors, functions and other operational details. Operating system software for computers is rarely in a finalised state and is constantly being updated and improved by the manufacturer. There is strict control over the distribution of amendments by the manufacturers who also provide managers of installations with advice and instructions on how the said amendments are to be implemented. A computer installation run in a professional manner will have tight documentary control over amendments, and management should know exactly which version of an operating system is running at a given time.

A claim that a given operating system is free from errors should never be taken seriously. Operating systems are tested by the supplier before delivery to the owners of the computer but errors can always be present which have not been detected by any of the tests carried out by the manufacturer. The likelihood of such errors being present in a given operating system decreases with time as it is used on various computer installations and errors are notified and rectified. Nevertheless it is always possible that an unusual set of circumstances may produce a computer error that was not discovered in the original testing procedures or spotted subsequently in use. The use of the 'latest release' of an operating system should be treated with caution until time (and progressively fewer errors) build up a level of confidence. More confidence can be placed in the accuracy of computer output emanating from a computer whose operating system and utility software (see below) have undergone several years of development than from a computer with a relatively new operating system and utilities, where the computer manufacturer may still be relying on usage to reveal errors.

'Utility software' is the name given to standard program routines which are frequently required by the user such as statistical utilities, record sorting and so on. Utilities can contain undetected errors, which are only produced under particular combinations of data. One case is worth recording.

A typical standard utility is one used to write (create) a new file on a new magnetic tape. To do this the file contents on the old magnetic tape mounted on one tape deck are 'updated' by being transferred under the control of the utility to a new magnetic tape mounted on another tape deck. The addition of new or changed records as the new magnetic tape is 'written' is under the control of the utility, which also keeps account of the records transferred. The utility is meant to produce an error message on the operator's console at the end of the process if, by means of a 'record count' test, all records have not been transferred. Owing to a latent error in the utility in the case considered some records on the old magnetic tape were not transferred to the new magnetic tape yet the count tallied so no error message was generated. Consequently the newly created magnetic tape was sent as an accurate record, of salaries due to employees, to a central banking clearing house. The error was not revealed until certain employees subsequently discovered that their accounts were not credited with sums of money due to them and made enquiries. The above error was produced by a rare double-fault condition.

Application software 'instructs' the computer to perform a specific task such as payroll calculations or stock control schedules. The means by which the programmer writes such software is described in full in Appendix A. This may be done in part either pictorially (by flowchart or decision table) or in narrative. The logical path through a program can be extremely complex and errors may be present in the original concept and subsequent specification. After writing the program the programmer should test it using specimen data. The programmer should then document his application program so that another programmer on looking at his program listing (the accepted name for the source form of a program) can understand the way he has undertaken the task. Errors can remain undetected in application software if one or more programs have been inadequately tested. Testing can only prove that errors exist. It is impossible by testing to prove that a complete program is completely free from errors. In a program with only 20 decision points there are more than 1,000,000 logical paths. Most programs have many more than 20 decision points.

Many computers only function correctly within prescribed temperature and humidity ranges and all only when supplied with electricity at the correct voltage and frequency and properly earthed. The large computers, or mainframes, are usually installed in specially built air-conditioned rooms which are controlled to meet stringent criteria. Most computers have warning and protection mechanisms to cope with failures in the actual environmental conditions but errors can be produced when these ranges are exceeded and before the warning mechanisms become effective. In addition dust, vibration and static electricity can affect their operation and may cause sporadic errors and corrupt output.

Throughout the world there is a trend towards geographically distributed processors (in effect, computer networks). In such networks, desk-top computer terminals can store and maintain a great deal of data and can communicate with other terminals attached to other computers as and when required. A problem can arise when a user at one terminal in a network makes an alteration to his copy of the common database. (A database is an organised collection of libraries of data.) An example can illustrate the problem.

Suppose a ticket agency has a local computer and terminal linked to a network of other local computer terminals in other ticket agencies. Each of the terminals has a copy of all the seats available at a certain London theatre. If the agent makes a booking he alters his local database. That alteration must be communicated to all the other locally stored databases. While that communication is circulating, another agent may make a booking and a clash of resources can result, producing deadlock – known as a deadly embrace. There are a variety of different techniques used in distributed processing to protect against this type of fault.

Extraneous electronic noise on data communication lines (the means of connecting network components) can produce errors. Checks are normally undertaken to stop data being corrupted but a trade-off between efficient use of communications lines and accuracy of data exists, which might cause commercial risk-taking. One of the most common error detection methods is parity checking, which tests whether the number of ones (or zeros) in an array of binary digits is odd or even. It is possible for parity detection systems to fail to operate correctly with resulting errors.

All computers, even micro systems, should be run in a professional manner. Where relevant, management should ensure that the computing processes are supervised and that the computer output does not contain latent errors. However, it is possible for unauthorised and not easily detectable modifications to be made to the hardware, programs and data in the computer, and management should ensure that the measures mentioned are implemented as a minimum standard.

Attention can be paid to division of responsibilities which is a traditional way of making fraud or tampering difficult. In computing environments, for example, programmers should not operate the computer; analysts should not authorise amendments; an independent observer should be present when output with a cash value (cheques) is being produced.

If a user replaces his computer with a machine from another manufacturer, his existing programs and data will have to be converted so as to run under a new operating system of a computer with a different logic design. During this period of conversion the computer will almost certainly produce errors. In a professionally-run installation a close watch will be maintained over the system for the first few months until all the errors have been corrected and the new system is running satisfactorily.

Any electronic, electro-mechanical or mechanical equipment can develop faults. Sometimes these are catastrophic and obvious (e.g. a bridge collapsing). In a sense this is the best kind of fault in that there can be no argument concerning its existence. In most cases concerning electronics, however, faults are intermittent so that the equipment works for some of the time and then for no obvious reason will fail, only to recover before an investigation into the cause of failure is successful. Sometimes the failure is of the kind typified by the faulty camera — the photographer will happily take a series of pictures, assuming his automatic aperture is working because the indicator says it is, only to find, days later on receipt of the processed film, that such was not the case. The fact that computers can fail in this way is particularly relevant to this book's theme.

The assembly of components that constitute a computer system do a job of work that is highly complex. They embrace advanced electronics, intricate electrical wiring, electro-mechanical devices that are at the limits of technology (e.g. the flying heads on magnetic disk drives), sophisticated cooling systems and stringent air-filtering. Computer manufacturers have learnt over the years to incorporate automatic and thorough self-checking techniques so that the state of all components can be monitored and appropriate warnings sounded when required. Indeed in some instances not only is a warning sounded but, to prevent actual damage to equipment or to prevent gross corruption of programs or data, the computer will automatically 'power down' or halt a computing process as appropriate.

Finally, in the context of errors it is useful to consider the computer working as a 'one-armed bandit' works. Every time the computer performs an operation it will check its pattern of ones and noughts at the end of the computation to see whether an error condition has developed. This is like the one-armed bandit checking to see if it has to pay out a winning combination of 'fruits'. Computers however have one major difference when compared with one-armed bandits — they perform the checking millions of times faster, and there is always a possibility that one particular combination of 'fruits' is missed by the double error which bypasses the error checking mechanism and results in an incorrect output. One of the jobs of computer staff should be to watch for and catch these latent errors, before the effect is felt by members of the public such as those employees who received no salary because the master tape did not contain their personal data.

There is always the possibility that the checking mechanisms have been 'doctored' so that they do not work in the way they should. Alterations of this kind to operating systems can be made by potential criminals. In short it is clear that while all computers — micros, minis and mainframes — have error checking and security features incorporated, it must not be assumed that these safeguards are infallible. It is also important to realise the ephemeral nature of the computational process and to this end essential evidence of, for example, function and malfunction should be collected and recorded continuously in a log, the said log perused from time to time by those responsible for the computer's operations and copies preserved for a finite period of time so that 'evidence' is always to hand.

CHAPTER THREE
Legal Matters

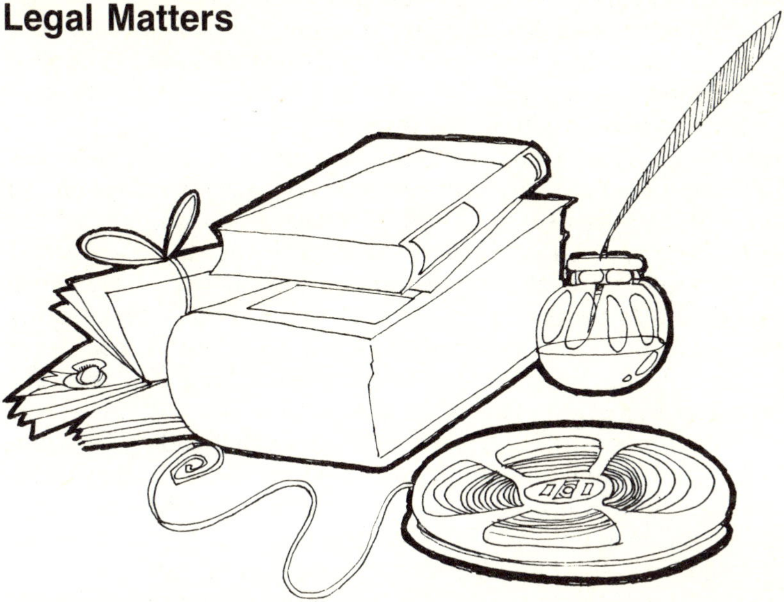

The law of evidence is a vast subject; the standard United States work is Wigmore which consists of ten volumes totalling more than 7,600 pages. In England the shortest text that does it justice is Cross on Evidence which runs to over 700 pages. The object of this chapter is to give the reader a thumbnail sketch of some of the areas where the apparent inadequacy of the law can be tested. References are made when appropriate to our imaginary case presented in chapters 4 to 7.

In criminal cases there are frequently arguments over whether the evidence against the accused is admissible in law and a great deal of time could be spent in deciding whether computer records are admissible. In *R. v Stevenson*[1] the court spent ten days on a trial within a trial deciding whether tape recordings between the accused and a prosecution witness were admissible. Tape recorders are simple devices; computers are not.

At least three matters should arise in considering the admis-

[1] [1971] 1 W.L.R.p1.

sibility of computer evidence. The first is whether the computer evidence is hearsay or real evidence and if it is hearsay, whether it is admissible as one of the exceptions to the hearsay rule. The reason for excluding hearsay evidence is rooted in the history of the common law trial. In the reign of Henry II some 800 years ago the common law trial was invented.

The single feature that distinguished an English common law trial from a trial elsewhere in Europe was cross-examination; an engine for the discovery of truth by tenacious questioning. After a couple of hundred years of trial and error the single feature of the common law trial engendered a technical rule: if evidence depends for its probative value upon the credibility of someone who cannot be cross-examined, it cannot be admitted because it runs foul of what was invented in the reign of Henry II, the right to cross-examination. This is the basis of the hearsay rule. Over the centuries the rule has been relaxed so that today there are many statutory and common law exceptions to the hearsay rule. Nevertheless a House of Lords case, *Myers v DPP*[2] held that the categories of common law exceptions to the hearsay rule are closed and it is for Parliament to expand them by statute.

In our imaginary case the Defence argument that the computer printout was hearsay and inadmissible under any of the statutory exceptions to the hearsay rule was based on *R. v Pettigrew*[3] the facts of which are outlined in Chapter 4. The prosecution's argument, that the computer evidence was real evidence was based on a case called the *Statue of Liberty*[4]. In the latter case it was held that the record made by a radar set by purely mechanical means without any human intervention was admissible to prove the movements of the ships and the place where the collision occurred. The then President of the Family Division giving the judgement of the court said, 'In my view the evidence in question in the present case has nothing to do with the hearsay rule and does not depend on the Evidence Act. . . .' If the *Statue of Liberty* is to be preferred to *Pettigrew* then, in the words of Professor Smith: 'Where information is recorded by mechanical means without the intervention of a human mind the record

[2] [1965] A.C. 1001.
[3] [1980] 71 G.App.R.39.
[4] [1968] 2 All E.R. 195.

made by the machine is admissible in evidence provided of course it is reliable.'[5]

However in a real case it may not always be a simple decision. For example many people today have cards which can be used in automatic bank terminals. These, when used, produce records which alter the balance noted in the statement. The other records in the statement are produced by human tellers processing the cheques of the account holder. The balance is therefore a hybrid derived from both kinds of records. In any case where strict rule of law was applied the judge would have to decide whether *Pettigrew*, a decision of a higher court than *Statue of Liberty*, would require him to rule that the balances given in bank statements are inadmissible.

The second matter concerns the reliability of computer evidence. The non-technical reader after reading Appendix A may begin to see that the exact workings of a large computer's operations in producing a particular printout would require an unacceptably long examination-in-chief. In practice, computer personnel testify as though they were experts expressing opinions about their computer system. This situation is only acceptable if those opinions are based on proper scientific analysis.

Program designing and coding can have a great deal in common with experimental scientific research or engineering design; all three have their share of design faults and errors, but in the last, a part of the instilled professional discipline is to organise and justify changes in design and error-correction procedures. Such practices are not yet widespread in the software aspects of the computing industry although determined efforts are being made by educational and professional bodies to introduce courses on 'software engineering', which imposes discipline on systems analysts and programmers.

The Data Processing Manager, when producing, as evidence, a printout from the computer he is in charge of, frequently says in a deposition that the computer was working properly. This is an opinion and, with a large and complex computer system, it is doubtful whether such a manager could have sufficient knowledge about the computer system to be capable of forming such an opinion based on fact. In an exhaustive analysis, different

[5] [1981] Criminal Law Review p.390, lines 7–11.

aspects of the computer may need to be considered, and a series of independent experts on hardware, software and communications may be required, with the Data Processing Manager merely testifying that no faults came to his notice at the particular time.

The selection of an expert is a very difficult task and there is no generally recognised 'expert' standard. The lawyer must therefore examine the qualifications and experience of each computer expert with considerable care.

Detailed information concerning the workings of a particular make of computer will be in the possession of the manufacturer of the computer. He will also have on his staff those most able to give expert testimony as to the workings of the computer. However, the manufacturer may know that a particular series of computers has a fault which he does not know how to fix, or does not choose to fix for a variety of commercial reasons. Such a manufacturer might not wish the fault in the computer to be discussed in open court with the associated publicity and it is sometimes useful to call in independent experts. In the United States there are several recorded cases of actions against manufacturers because of secret faults in their computer systems. In the case of imported systems discovery proceedings outside the jurisdiction are not very practical; cross-examination of experts must be undertaken tenaciously.

What is called the 'best evidence' rule has declined greatly in importance over recent years. The rule rejects inferior evidence such as a copy of a document, or a witness's description of an object if the original is obtainable. Nonetheless the rule still applies to tape recordings[1] and by analogy could apply to computer evidence. Thus a judge may require the original printout from the computer's control console rather than a printout produced by the same console at a later date reproducing the same information. The problem arises that in many cases the two may look identical. It will be up to the court to lay down conditions for the admissibility of these records, taking into account the security procedures used in the computer installation.

The best evidence problem in computers may be illustrated by the following tale. A man was employed as a security adviser to a bank in the mid-west of America. One day, as a security alertness test he got permission from the President of another bank in the area to forge a Telex from the said President to the

President of his employer's bank. The Telex said, 'We have just arrested one of our employees for embezzlement. He put an illegal patch in the computer system. He says he learnt the technique from employees at your bank who were doing the same thing 18 months ago.' The security adviser took the forged Telex and showed it to the Data Processing Manager who naturally became extremely worried. He realised immediately that whilst it was possible to show that a particular suite of programs had been loaded onto the computer three years ago and that a suite that appeared identical was running on the computer at the time, it was not possible to show what programs were running 18 months ago.

As a result a complex security procedure was developed by the adviser so that it was possible to demonstrate, *inter alia*, that the system had not been tampered with. Whether a computer system is secure against tampering should be the modern version of the best evidence rule. Forthcoming privacy legislation will probably require that computer users comply with some minimum security requirements and these could form the basis of best evidence argument.

In civil cases the statutory exceptions to the hearsay rule are contained in a more up-to-date statute, the Civil Evidence Act 1968. Section 5 of the Act was drafted explicitly to cater for the admissibility of computer records. However, the wording of the Act reflects the state-of-the-art 15 years ago. A computer is defined in section 5(6) as 'any device for storing and processing information'. This appears to mean the hardware and no mention is made of software anywhere in the Act. For a computer printout to be admissible in a civil case, the following conditions need to be satisfied. The computer printout has to have been produced by the computer during a period over which the computer was used regularly to store or to process information for the purposes of any activity regularly carried on over that period; over the period there was regularly supplied to the computer in the ordinary course of those activities, information of the kind contained in the statement or of the kind from which the information so contained is derived; throughout the material part of that period the computer must have been operating properly; and the information contained in the statement reproduces or is derived from information supplied to the computer in the ordinary course of those activities.

This wide and detailed definition contains hidden flaws. First it might exclude computer output which is not regularly generated. If a computer is used for accounting purposes, the programs which are used to check to see whether the computer is being misused are run very occasionally. On a strict interpretation of this section, an interpretation supported by *Myers v DDP*, occasional computer audit evidence might be excluded. Many of the most important computer outputs are not produced regularly but only in response to a particular need or question. Nowadays this may well apply to the console log; in many modern systems no hard copy is produced unless requested, the information being recorded on a disk file. The fourth requirement, that the information contained in the statement reproduces or is derived from information supplied to the computer in the ordinary course of those activities, does not appear to cover the computer logs just mentioned. These are printouts of information supplied *by* the computer from sources known to itself alone. The order number and the time from the real-time clock in our imaginary case are both pieces of information that were supplied by machine action alone. A pedantic argument is also possible because of the choice of words in the Act. The Act uses the word information in the wrong sense — it really means data.[6] The figure 170 can be termed an item of data. The information conveyed by the data is intangible and dependent on many other factors. Thus the phrase 'Apple Corporation grew at 170% in 1980' turns the data

[6] Data and information are different from each other. The former is tangible, the latter intangible. When discussing computer systems it is usually necessary to distinguish between them. However the distinction is not strictly germane to the main purpose of the book but the following extract from the Report of the Data Protection Committee, page 150, can be noted.

> 'Information is the knowledge conveyed to the mind by a statement of fact, and it is not therefore susceptible of ownership. Where the statement is contained in a document, or other object having physical existence, that object is capable of being owned like any other chattel; but there is no ownership in the knowledge (true or false) which the document can be used to convey. The nearest that the law approaches to treating a complex of ideas as a form of property is in the law of copyright. But even there, all that the law does is to prohibit people from exploiting the work in question in certain specified ways without the leave of the copyright owner. Moreover, copyright does not go to the knowledge conveyed: newspapers frequently publish information culled from other newspapers.'

into information. The computing equivalent of the 'angels on the head of a pin' argument can be found in the frequent technical arguments concerning the meaning of the term 'information'.

The Civil Evidence Act 1972 made provision for the admissibility in evidence of statements of opinion. Section 1(1) specifically excluded evidence from computers as opinion evidence. While this may be the case today, a new programming technique developed from work in the area of robotics and machine intelligence indicates that opinion evidence from computers may become a possibility. Most computers, as explained in Appendix A, solve problems by algorithmic techniques. For any given input there is only one computational path through the program to the solution. Such a computer cannot be said to have opinions. However, in Britain and in the United States there has been a considerable amount of research and development into an heuristic method of problem solving in computer systems.

Computers that solve problems by heuristic techniques are termed 'expert systems' and have already been used in America for predicting good drilling sites in the exploration for rare minerals, for assisting doctors in diagnosis and for help in the recognition of molecular structure from the results of mass spectrographs. The expert system is geared particularly to solving problems where there is a large body of expertise to be drawn on. Inside the system there are two parts; a corpus of knowledge and a mechanism for applying the knowledge in an heuristic way to the solution of the problems called an 'inference engine'. This mechanism 'strikes sparks' in the knowledge section, couples parts of the knowledge together and finds opportunistic paths through the computations.

Expert systems will find uses in the 1980s in process control and in areas such as collision avoidance in aircraft, ships and possibly, motor cars. Expert systems will be able to give a reasoned opinion concerning the existence or otherwise of facts. Courts may have to decide whether it is negligent to override an expert system that is flying an aircraft or controlling a production line. The expert system could give its reasons for a particular course of action but understanding the logic and argument that lead to the said action could take several hours or days of studying a computer printout in a special form called 'hexadecimal' described in Appendix A.

The development of expert systems may cause the legal practitioner further problems. The testimony from an expert system will be derived from information supplied to the computer from sources known to itself alone (e.g. real-time clocks) and information derived by the computer by use of the inference engine. The inference engine contains programs that change dynamically as the computer learns in accordance with the original programs supplied by a human programmer. Lawyers will therefore be faced with the problem of cross-examining an inference engine programmer on the correctness of the original programs supplied to the expert system and from which it had dynamically learnt.

For the above reasons there seems to be a strong case to consider revising the Civil Evidence Acts. The 11th Report of the Criminal Law Revision Committee on Evidence (General) (CMND 4991) recommended that a clause similar to Section 5 of the Civil Evidence Act 1968 be enacted in a new Criminal Evidence Act. This seems unsatisfactory. The present lack of clarity caused by *Pettigrew* and the *Statue of Liberty* does not assist anyone. Nobody knows what the House of Lords might say in a hybrid case. Until then it is worth mentioning that in the key case *Myers*, the House of Lords were unanimous in the opinion that the evidence in question was hearsay, whereas the Court of Criminal Appeal considered that it was not.

Readers are correct if they question whether the use of a video recording of a confravision conversation as described in Chapter 7 would be admissible. One serious objection to admitting the evidence of one of our characters, Cherry Cheesecake, is that if she is committing perjury she does so outside the jurisdication of the court. It is doubtful whether she could be extradited from the United States or whether a court would be satisfied that the person giving evidence was Miss Cheesecake unless there was independent identification.

Finally in this chapter we quote from the Australian Law Reform Commission Research Paper No 3 on hearsay evidence, page 165 — Telecommunications:

> The rule against hearsay evidence prevents messages in the form of Telexes, teleprinter, and telefacsimile being tendered by the recipient to prove the fact that the message

was sent by the person purporting to be the sender to the person to whom it is addressed.

Those planning to make use of electronic mail should remember that the Common Law is the same in both Britain and Australia and thus the hearsay rule would prevent a document (say a valuable order for goods to be manufactured) being tendered by a recipient to prove the fact that the document was sent by the person purporting to be the sender to the person to whom it is addressed if the document had been sent by electronic mail. The present evidence statutes are now fruitful sources of technical arguments, and the need for new evidence legislation is apparent if we are to make best use of information technology.

In the next chapter we outline the facts of our computer evidence case and indicate how it might proceed from the time when an accused is charged to his appearing in a Crown Court.

CHAPTER FOUR

The Computer as a Witness I

The Case of Grapefruit Sorbet

Cornet Supermarkets in 1982 installed a laser checkout system which reads the bar codes (those funny lines of varying thickness) on packets of groceries. As customers' groceries were scanned the sale was automatically noted on the till which printed out a detailed receipt and logged the sale in a local computer. This, in turn, communicated with a central computer at headquarters to provide information for re-ordering.[1] Cornet Supermarkets also had a special telephone order service whereby an order was taken by an operator at headquarters and then sent electronically to a branch near the customer where it was made up, wrapped, addressed and delivered by van. The customer paid by quoting the number of a store credit card over the telephone at the time the order was placed.[2]

[1] This is not science fiction; all the major supermarket chains in Britain have stores where they are testing out laser scanners for bar-code reading.
[2] This is an established practice in many 'up-market' stores.

Mr Grapefruit Sorbet was a shelf-filler at a branch of Cornet Supermarkets. He was eighteen years old, popular and ambitious, attending evening classes at his local polytechnic in electronic data processing, and planned to become a computer operator. On Thursday, January 23 he had an argument with the manager because of time he had spent in the computer terminal room developing a program that was part of his evening class studies. He refused to promise that he wouldn't do it again so the manager suggested that he work out the rest of the week and then leave. Grapefruit agreed and left at 5.00 p.m. on Saturday after collecting his pay and cards. On arriving home he found a package on his doorstep from Cornet Supermarkets, which on opening he found to contain two bottles of champagne, some tinned oysters, fillet steak and a jar of Beluga caviar — all wrapped up and bearing the machine-printed label giving his name and address. Thinking it was a farewell gift from his friends on the staff at the supermarket he and his girlfriend later ate the steak, oysters and caviar and drank the champagne. On the Monday he telephoned one of his friends at the supermarket intending to ask him to thank the staff for their gift but was told that they had not sent him one.

On the Tuesday a policeman arrived to ask him some questions. It later transpired that according to the computer record maintained by Cornet Supermarkets, Grapefruit had ordered groceries by telephone and had them charged up as stocktaking loss items so that no invoice was generated. Grapefruit could offer no explanation as to how his address had appeared on the list of completed orders. The police charged Grapefruit with theft of the groceries late the same afternoon.

Normal police procedure was followed; Grapefruit was allowed bail without surety because he had no criminal record.[3] The case came up on the following Monday before magistrates where it was adjourned while Grapefruit was granted legal aid, and the prosecution prepared the case against him. Grapefruit meanwhile saw his solicitor who advised him that he should have the matter tried in the Crown Court rather than being tried in the magistrates court because there were complex questions of law and

[3] For a readable guide to criminal procedure see *The Criminal Court in Action* by David Bernard; Butterworths 1979.

there was a higher chance of an acquittal before a jury. The solicitor who had been sent copies of the statements took the view that on these statements there was a case to answer and Grapefruit should apply for a formal committal for trial in the Crown Court so that the magistrates did not have to look at the evidence.[4] Committal proceedings occurred in the Magistrates Court two weeks later and bail was renewed without surety. Grapefruit's solicitor prepared a brief to counsel containing the statements tendered at the committal and Grapefruit's version of events. Grapefruit's counsel, Mr Honey-Bunny then worked on these papers, had a conference with Grapefruit, looked up the law and prepared the case for trial.

The Trial of Grapefruit Sorbet
(Barnet Crown Court, December 5th 1983 10.30 a.m.)

Usher:	All rise. *The judge enters, everyone bows and the judge sits down.*
Clerk of the Court:	Put up Grapefruit Sorbet. *Mr Sorbet is led into the dock.* Is your name Grapefruit Sorbet?
G.S.	Yes.
Clerk:	Grapefruit Sorbet you are charged in an indictment with obtaining property by deception contrary to section 15 of the Theft Act 1968 the particulars of the offence being that you, on the 25th day of January 1983 without lawful excuse obtained property by deception, namely fillet steak, oysters, Beluga caviar and champagne belonging to Cornet Supermarkets Limited. To the charge do you plead guilty or not guilty?
G.S.	Not guilty. *Mr Honey-Bunny, counsel for the defence, stands up.*
H.B.	Your Honour, before the jury is empanelled I have a motion to quash the indictment concerning the admissibility of a key piece of the prosecution's evi-

[4] This may have been a mistake on the part of the solicitor in view of the arguments at the Crown Court hearing regarding admissibility of evidence from computers.

dence relating to the charge. Has your Honour had an opportunity of reading the depositions?

Judge: I have been able to glance through the statements — are you sure Mr Honey-Bunny that this is the right time to make such an application? The prosecution has not opened their case and they might not rely on the statement you object to.

H.B. Your Honour, I have already spoken to my learned friend and he will be relying on this key piece of evidence; it is at the heart of the case. If I am successful in this application it is likely that the charge against my client will have to be dropped for lack of evidence and all the time taken in swearing-in a jury will have been saved.

Judge: Mr Toffee-Almond, what are your views on this?

Mr Toffee-Almond, counsel for the prosecution, stands up.

T.A. There are complex legal issues, your Honour, and we might well take the rest of this morning arguing them. I agree with my learned friend that this may be the time to deal with them though I reserve my position at this point on the question of costs.

Judge Thank you Mr Toffee-Almond. Mr Honey-Bunny you may proceed.

H.B. I am much obliged your Honour. I refer to the statement of Mr Sandwich, the data processing manager of Cornet Supermarkets. In this statement he says that an order was made up on the day in question for the groceries supplied to Mr Sorbet. He makes this statement by reference to an order listing produced by the Cornet Supermarkets computer system. Each record on the listing consists of three numbers — the time, the order number and the customer reference number. I submit, your Honour, that this statement is hearsay and is not admissible under one of the exceptions to the hearsay rule. Mr Sandwich's statement is founded upon this hearsay statement and is therefore also inadmissible.

Judge: Your argument therefore is based on the admissibility of computer evidence?

H.B. That's right, in particular on the admissibility of automatically generated computer evidence. It might help at this point if I cite my first case, *the Queen against Pettigrew*,[5] a decision of the Court of Criminal Appeal. The case concerned a burglary in the north of England. A house was broken into and some money was stolen. The money consisted of £650 in new £5 notes that had been supplied to the victim of the burglary by a local branch of the Trustee Savings Bank. The police arrested Mr Stewart Pettigrew. At the time of his arrest three new £5 notes were found in his possession. At the trial the prosecution attempted to put in as evidence a computer printout from the Bank of England that identified the serial numbers of a bundle of some £5,000 worth of notes that had been sent from the Bank of England to a bank in Newcastle, parts of which could be specifically traced through the local branch of the Trustee Savings Bank and into the possession of the victim of the burglary.

This evidence suggested that the three new £5 notes found in Pettigrew's possession when arrested might have come from the same series of notes that had been given to the victim by his bank. The prosecution, with the jury absent, placed the printout in evidence pursuant to the provisions of the Criminal Evidence Act 1965, Section One. *Mr Honey-Bunny lifts a paper from his table and read out*:

> In any criminal proceedings where direct oral evidence of a fact would be admissible, any statement contained in a document and tending to establish that fact shall, on production of the document, be admissible as evidence of that fact if —
>
> (a) the document is, or forms part of, a record relating to any trade or business and com-

[5] [1980] 71C. App. Rep. 39. When citing a case counsel usually produces the approved law report, reads the headnote (synopsis) and the parts of the judgement he relies on. This we cannot do for copyright reasons.

> piled, in the course of that trade or business, from information supplied (whether directly or indirectly) by persons who have, or may reasonably be supposed to have, personal knowledge of the matters dealt with in the information they supply . . .

Your Honour, Counsel for Pettigrew objected to this printout being put in evidence on the ground that the Bank of England was not a trade or business. The learned judge overruled that objection, the printout was put in evidence and Pettigrew was convicted.

Judge: I fail to see the relevance of any of this, Mr Honey-Bunny.

H.B. It will become clear in a moment your Honour. Pettigrew appealed against his conviction and in the Court of Appeal his defence counsel raised a different objection to the computer printout being put in evidence. He said that the information recorded in the computer printout was not information supplied by any person who had or could reasonably be supposed to have had personal knowledge of the matters dealt with in the information. The Court of Appeal in exploring this point had to consider how the printout came into being.

The printout came from a machine which counted and checked newly printed bank notes. An operator took a bundle of a hundred new notes, noted the first serial number of the bundle on a card and fed them into the machine. The machine noted the serial numbers of the first and last notes in the bundle, had a look at each note in turn and rejected those it thought were bad, noting down their serial numbers. It finally outputted the bundle, which contained notes running consecutively in series, save only in so far as the machine had rejected certain notes.

Judge: The relevance of your submission is still not clear.

H.B. It should become apparent in just a minute, your Honour. Their Lordships after due deliberation held that the numbers on the notes which are regarded as having been rejected could never be said to be in the personal knowledge of the operator or in the mind of anybody. One could impute knowledge to the machine but the operator could never be said to have had knowledge of the rejected notes. Pettigrew was acquitted and the Court of Appeal expressed the view that the point was highly technical and exposed a gap in the Criminal Evidence Act 1965.

Judge: Very good Mr Honey-Bunny, now what is the relevance in this case?

H.B. Mr Sandwich has deposed and will doubtless state in evidence that the goods in question were ordered at 4.23 on the Friday afternoon. Mr Sandwich made this statement by looking at computer-generated printout which, I submit, is inadmissible evidence as hearsay and is not covered by the statutory exemption in the Criminal Evidence Act 1965. The time and the order number, both highly relevant to the interests of the defendant, are automatically generated by the computer itself and not as the result of a human operator.

Judge: Can you be a little more explicit, Mr Honey-Bunny?

H.B. I'll try, your Honour. As you know from reading through the depositions Cornet Supermarkets have a telephone order service. A customer telephones the head office and a telephone operator equipped with a computer terminal takes the call.

The customer gives an account number and the operator types this in. A personal question appears on the screen, normally something like 'What day is your mother's birthday?' and the operator reads this out and types in the reply from the customer. If the correct answer is given the operator takes the customer's order, and by typing commands at a keyboard, debits it to the customer's account and types in the address to which it is to be sent if this differs from the normal account address. The order is then transmitted to the nearest local supermarket for make-up, labelling and despatch. Now, when the operator gets the right answer to the question (the validation), the computer automatically assigns a number to the order that is about to be typed in, an order number. This number does not appear on the screen. It would only confuse the operator and is taken from a set of numbers on file in the computer. When the order has been typed in, the computer checks that goods are all available at the local supermarket and that the value of the order does not exceed the customer's credit rating. It then calculates the time of day from an internal device called a real-time clock, and makes an internal record which consists of three numbers: the time of day, the order number and the customer number. These are printed out later as required.

I submit your Honour, that on the printout so obtained neither the time of day nor the order number is admissible as evidence because they are not pieces of information supplied by persons who may reasonably be supposed to have personal knowledge of the matters dealt with in the information they supply. They are pieces of information generated by machine action alone and are outside the class of admissible hearsay evidence. Since Mr Sandwich's deposition is based totally on this hearsay evidence it is inadmissible.

Judge: I see Mr Honey-Bunny. Mr Toffee-Almond, what do you have to say? Mr Honey-Bunny's arguments are logically attractive — we cannot get the computer to come into this court, take the oath and testify; or can we?

T.A. No, your Honour, but I think we can distinguish the present case from Pettigrew. First of all I submit that a computer gives real evidence and not hearsay evidence, in the same way that a bloodstained knife found at the scene of a murder gives fingerprints. You cannot cross-examine an inanimate object like a knife but you can get an expert to examine the object and express a professional opinion about it.

Judge:

So what is your view of the Pettigrew case?

T.A. I feel that the prosecution approached the problem the wrong way. An expert should have been called to give opinion evidence concerning the note-counting computer, testifying as to the working conditions and the reliance that could be put on it. The expert could then have placed the computer printout in evidence in support of his testimony. I propose to place the Cornet Supermarkets' printout in evidence by the same means, as real evidence.[6]

Judge: Mr Honey-Bunny, do you wish to reply?

H.B. Yes, your Honour. It is settled law that expert evidence must be based on admissible evidence.[7] An opinion given by an expert based on his examination of hearsay testimony is not admissible. Let me put it this way. Suppose I wanted to prove that a fingerprint was that of the accused in a murder case. My learned friend suggests that I could call an expert to testify that he had conducted a delphic poll of a series of Home Office approved forensic examiners who had seen the fingerprint and believed that it was that of the accused. You, your Honour, would exclude such testimony on classical grounds, stating that although such evidence was admissible as to the beliefs of the Home Office experts it was not admissible as to the maker of the fingerprint. The computer believed that the time of 4.23 p.m., the account number and the order number in question are associated. English law has always excluded evidence where the deponent was unable to be cross-examined because cross-examination distils truth from opinion. Computers cannot be cross-examined; I cannot distil truth from a mass of silicon chips.

Judge: Yes, Mr Honey-Bunny, but computers unlike humans do not express opinions,[8] they state facts. In this case we are dealing with two facts; an order

[6] For further analysis of Pettigrew see Smith, J. C. Criminal Law Review, June 1981 pp.387–391.

[7] *Cross on Evidence*, 5th Edition, 446 para 2.

[8] On whether the judge is wrong and computers can express opinions, see section on expert systems in Chapter 3.

number and a time of day, both of which were produced by the computer automatically.

H.B. I know, your Honour, but they are not pure facts capable of interpretation, they are derived facts. The computer has taken raw data and at a given time has processed it producing information which it offers to us as facts.

Judge: Yes, but it has derived the information from the data by following a logical process in a program. A computer cannot have an off-day,[9] be caught with a hangover or feel malice towards a defendant. True, it derives the information from the data but it does so in a precise, reproducible manner according to instructions contained in programs. I feel that you have an interesting argument that may form part of the grounds for an appeal against a conviction, if that proves necessary, but I do not totally exclude the evidence just on a technical argument. Shall we swear the jury in?

[9] A computer clearly cannot have an 'off-day'' as a human being can, but it can be wrong as is explained in Appendix B.

CHAPTER FIVE
The Computer as a Witness II

(A jury has now been sworn in.)

Clerk of the Court: Members of the jury. The defendant, Grapefruit Sorbet stands charged in an indictment with obtaining property by deception contrary to Section 15 of the Theft Act 1968, the particulars of the offence being that he on the 24th day of January 1983, without lawful excuse obtained property by deception namely fillet steak, oysters, Beluga caviar and champagne, belonging to Cornet Supermarkets. It is your charge, members of the jury, having heard the evidence to say whether he be guilty or not guilty.

Judge: Yes, Mr Toffee-Almond.

T.A. May it please your Honour, members of the jury, I appear in this case for the prosecution and my learned friend Mr Honey-Bunny represents the defendant. You have heard the charge against Grapefruit Sorbet, the obtaining of some expensive groceries by deception. It is now my task to explain to you what the prosecution seek to prove against Mr Sorbet but, before I do, let me say that in this case as in every criminal trial it is for the prosecution to prove the case against the defendant and prove the case so that you are satisfied that you feel sure of guilt. If you are finally left in doubt then you acquit the defendant.

Mr Sorbet was employed by Cornet Supermarkets. On Thursday, 23rd January, the manager terminated his employment to be effective from the Saturday. Late on the afternoon of Friday, 24th January, an order was placed on the computer system that resulted in the expensive groceries being delivered to Mr Sorbet's home address on Saturday, 25th January, with the charge being billed as a stocktaking loss. The case for the prosecution is simply that it was Mr Sorbet himself who placed the order in the computer intending to obtain the property, groceries, without paying for them. If, after hearing the evidence you find those facts proved you must find the defendant guilty. And now with his Honour's permission, I shall call the evidence before you. Call Pablo Picashew.

Mr Pablo Picashew, the store manager is called and sworn in.

T.A. . . . Mr Picashew, you are the supermarket manager at the branch of Cornet Supermarkets where Mr Sorbet worked?

P.P. Yes.

T.A. Could you tell the court what happened on Thursday, January 23rd, in the supermarket?

P.P. Yes, I fired Grapefruit Sorbet for . . .[1]

[1] Mr Picashew wants to say that he fired Mr Sorbet for using the store terminal to develop his programs. This evidence is highly prejudicial and goes only to knowledge of computing rather than the facts in issue. If the prosecution get this in now the defence could apply to have the jury dismissed and ask for a retrial. The matter will only arise if the defence put in issue the question of whether Grapefruit Sorbet had the technical ability to work the system. At this stage the prosecution do not know whether the defence will call Mr Sorbet to testify.

T.A. That's fine, Mr Picashew, about what time did you fire him?

P.P. It was just after two. I know since I had come back from lunch and found him . . .

T.A. That's fine, Mr Picashew. Now what happened subsequently?

P.P. I don't understand.

H.B. As far as the defence is concerned there is no dispute that Mr Sorbet was not on the supermarket floor at around four p.m. on Friday, January 24th, so I have no objection if my learned friend leads Mr Picashew on these matters.

Judge: Thank you Mr Honey-Bunny.

T.A. I am grateful to my learned friend. Now, did you try and find Mr Sorbet around four p.m. that afternoon?

P.P. Yes, I put out several Tannoy announcements and I even asked the till girls to tell him I wanted to see him again.

T.A. Why did you wish to see him?

P.P. I wanted to try to reason with him. I felt that if he apologised and agreed not to use the terminal again then . . .[2]

T.A. Thank you, Mr Picashew. When did he finally appear?

P.P. At ten to five he walked into my office. I asked him where he had been and why he had not answered before.

T.A. What did he say?

P.P. He became abusive, said he had been working and had only just heard the Tannoy request.

T.A. Are all the Tannoy speakers working?

P.P. All except the one speaker in the room containing the computer terminals.

T.A. Can staff leave the store during the working day?

P.P. Only by going through Security Control. Because of pilfering there are guards on every exit who are required to stop all staff leaving during shop hours.

[2] As it turns out the defence either miss this point or do not choose to make an issue of it. This is probably correct because of the attitude of the judge.

The Security Officer had no record of him leaving. I'd already checked.

T.A. So Mr Sorbet must have been in the store at the time you called him?

P.P. Yes.

T.A. How many Tannoy messages did you put out?

P.P. Three. One just after four, one just before four-thirty and one at just after quarter to five.

T.A. So he came in response to your third Tannoy request and said he had not heard the first two?

P.P. Yes.

T.A. Are there any other places other than the terminal room where you cannot hear Tannoy messages?

P.P. No, it's the only place in the store.

T.A. Thank you. Your witness.

H.B. I have no questions to put to Mr Pablo Picashew.

The prosecution have shown by the above testimony, which has not been disputed, that Mr Sorbet was somewhere in the store between four and four-thirty, but could not be found. His statement to Mr Picashew that he had not heard the Tannoy announcement at just after four and just before four-thirty is slight circumstantial evidence indicating that during that period he might have been in the terminal room.

T.A. I call Professor Chocolate Chip.

The Usher calls Professor Chip who takes the stand and is sworn in.

T.A. Is your name Professor Chocolate Chip?

C.C. Yes.

T.A. And are you Professor of Surrealist Mathematics at Neasden University?

C.C. Yes.

T.A. Before you took up your present appointment you held the chair in Information System Design at the University of Hollywood in California?

C.C. That is correct.

T.A. Would it be true to say that you are considered to be an expert on computers and computer systems?

C.C. Yes.

T.A. The U.S. Department of Defense has sought your professional opinion from time to time?

C.C. Yes, on a number of national defence matters.

T.A. Now, you have examined the computer system employed by Cornet Supermarkets?

C.C. Yes, it is a Kamikaze DDB7 with an Asthma operating system and a specially-written suite of application programs by Spaghetti Supermarket Software.

T.A. Would all three result in a reliable computer system?

C.C. Yes, very reliable. Kamikaze Computers have been making computers for fifty-odd years and their products have been used throughout the world by governments, commerce and industry. The Asthma operating system is sound, and the Spaghetti Company is known internationally as a reputable software house.

T.A. Do you have any reason to think that the Cornet Supermarkets' computer system was not working properly and was producing inaccurate results?

C.C. On the contrary, I have every faith in the Cornet computer system. Especially after the numerous checks I ran on it.

T.A. Tell the court about those checks.

C.C. Well, I was asked to explain how the computer produced the output that it did, covering Friday and Saturday orders and delivery schedules. To do so I performed an on-site investigation by a method known as simulation. I looked at the way the computer was used, put in some fictitious test data and checked the various outputs produced. Inside the computer is an electronic clock that is used to log the time of day at which an event takes place, together with the date. I checked the functioning of the clock and the date mechanism and found them to be accurate. Next I put in a sample series of orders against real and fictitious account numbers logging the time of insertion by checking them against the computer's clock display of time and my watch. In all experiments the computer worked perfectly and the output records and messages on the console log and the line printer listings were correct.

T.A. Your Honour, could the witness be shown the first printout?

C.C. *Shown the printout.* Yes, that is the printout of my experiments. The handwritten figures down the side indicate the time and the order number I predicted, which should have been selected by the computer. As you can see there were no errors in over thirty results and the log and the listing correspond.

Judge: Let's call that set Exhibit 1 and Exhibit 2.

T.A. Now, can you tell me about your simulations?

C.C. Yes, I had tried and failed to order goods using a fictitious account number. I found however that the computer would accept a particular number, the stocktaking loss account number, without complaint.

T.A. Can you elaborate on this?

C.C. Certainly. For database design reasons loss of stock is treated as a customer account. I found that if I typed in the loss account number the computer accepted this as a valid shop account and I was able to order goods to any value. There was one little snag though.

T.A. Oh, what was that?

C.C. I had to answer a validating question.

T.A. What was the validating question?

C.C. It was rather an odd one. The computer asked, 'What is my mother's name?'

T.A. Why was that not the normal sort of validity question?

C.C. It was odd because the question was not the normal way round. Normally the computer asked what *your* relative's name is rather than requesting information about its own antecedents. The correct answer in this case was 'Cherry'.

T.A. Your Honour, could the witness be shown the second printout?

C.C. *Shown the printout.* Yes, those are the simulation results.

T.A. From your investigations can you suggest how the evidence against Mr Sorbet came into existence?

C.C. In my opinion that evidence could only have been created by a person at a terminal ordering goods using the stock-loss code.

T.A. Thank you Professor Chocolate Chip. Wait there. Your witness.

H.B. Professor Chocolate Chip, you say you conducted extensive tests on the computer system using simulation techniques and your watch?

C.C. That's right.

H.B. When did you conduct these tests?

C.C. Between April 7th and 10th.

H.B. I see. You tested the computer three months after it had made the records with which we are concerned?

C.C. Yes, and it worked perfectly.

H.B. But we are not concerned about how it worked when you tested it, we are looking to how it behaved on January 24th and 25th. Now you are obviously familiar with console logs as you mentioned them when replying to my learned friend's questions?

C.C. Yes.

H.B. Will you explain to the court please what such a log is used for?

C.C. A console log is used to check on the correct operation of the computer — it records time continuously and shows other information, for example when hardware and software errors occur.

H.B. Were you able to obtain the logs for the relevant periods, January 24th and 25th?

C.C. Most of them. There was a period of several hours on two occasions for which the log appeared to be missing.

H.B. Were you able to determine how many faults had occurred?

C.C. Yes. Between January and April the log showed four events — two close together, the others some time later — and I was able to see from the operator's diary that they resulted in routine service calls.

H.B. What happened on each occasion?

C.C. Well, on the first two the engineers found a faulty visual display unit used by the operator and a faulty disk channel. On the VDU the terminal screen was flickering. They changed it for a new one. A faulty disk drive was also changed. The third time the computer tripped out because of overheating. This was traced to a faulty fan. The last time an operator spilled a cup of coffee into the line printer, which needed a new tractor mechanism, printer barrel and ribbon.

H.B. So the computer you tested in April had a new operator terminal, disk drive, cooling fan and parts of a line printer?

C.C. Yes, so what?

H.B. Please let me continue. Now, the Kamikaze computer system uses an Asthma operating system?

C.C. Yes.

H.B. What version of the operating system was running on the computer on the date you tested it?

C.C. Version 2.6.

H.B. And what version was running on January 24th and 25th?

C.C. So far as I can tell it was version 2.6.

H.B. Why can you not be certain?

C.C. The console log is missing for a period of several hours so I have had to rely on the operator's diary which shows that version 2.6 was loaded at about 06.00 on the 24th.

H.B. Is the console log considered to be of importance?

C.C. It depends. When a real-time system has been running successfully for some time then the log is of little interest. In batch it's essential.

H.B. But if a new version of an operating system in a real-time and batch environment had been installed would it not be useful?

C.C. I would say essential. There are bound to be some latent errors during the first few hours and the messages on the console log are often the only clues in any investigation.

H.B. I am informed by the Kamikaze company that version 2.6 of Asthma had been found to have an error in the way in which it handled files and that all owners had been Telexed on January 23rd to revert to 2.4. So, Professor Chocolate Chip, it is likely that 2.4 was running on the 24th and 25th and not 2.6?

Judge: Mr Honey-Bunny, what are you trying to show?

H.B. I am trying to prove, your Honour, that Professor Chocolate Chip did not test the computer that produced the so-called evidence on January 24th and 25th. So far I have shown that the computer he tested had different hardware and now I have shown that he is unaware of which operating system was running. As the operating system determines how the hardware and the application programs interact, a change in operating system is an entirely new machine. As the logs are missing it cannot be proved one way or the other but the Kamikaze Telex suggests it should have been 2.4 to avoid the possibility of file-handling errors with 2.6.

C.C. But none of the hardware changes could conceivably have produced any different result.

H.B. What about the difference between the versions of the operating system?

C.C. Version 2.6 is almost identical to Version 2.4.

H.B. But the Kamikaze company Telexed users about a major difference, and a fault at that.

C.C. Yes, but they had only restructured the file-handling capability by using a different algorithm and it must have been a fault in that area.

Judge: I see.

Silence.

H.B. What do you mean by restructuring?

C.C. They changed the way in which records are sorted.

H.B. Professor Chocolate Chip, are you telling this court that Version 2.6 sorts account records and order records in a different way from version 2.4?

C.C.

Well, yes, I am.

H.B. And this case turns on an account record and an order record being sorted. This is now done differently?

C.C. Yes, but whether Version 2.4 or 2.6 was used, I would still have got the same result.

H.B. That is your unsupported opinion. Your testimony is irrelevant because you did not test the computer in question.

Judge: Why, Professor Chocolate Chip, do you think you would have produced identical results if you had tested the computer system?

C.C. Because the fault which allows goods to be charged against stock-loss is not in the operating system, it is in the application program.

H.B. Are you certain it is a fault?

C.C. Well, it must be a fault; no system designer would allow that to happen.

H.B. Professor, I would now like to turn to the validation dialogue. You told this court that the question was posed the wrong way round and that the correct answer was 'Cherry'.

C.C. That's right.

H.B. How did you discover what the correct answer was?

C.C. I looked at the system dump.

Silence.

Judge: You mean, . . . er, . . . Professor, what on earth do you mean?

C.C. I looked at the system dump listing. I obtained the master password from Mr Sandwich and got a print-out of all the validation dialogue and files from the historical records relevant to the time and date of the alleged offence. The line printer produced that pile of documents over there.

Judge: Which one?

C.C. The pile of printout to the left of Mr Toffee-Almond; the pile that's about three and a half feet high.

Judge: I think I had better come down to look at it rather than getting the Usher to pass it up to me — you might not see me again for the rest of the trial. *Laughter. The judge gets down, walks over to the* *printout and looks at the top sheet of the fan-folded document.*

Judge: *He reads out the first line.* 'C9 eleven A2 6B'. This is nonsense!

C.C. Almost right, your Honour. It is not nonsense, but it may be garbage. As you know, the computer thinks in ones and noughts and the first figure you stated, 'C9' is actually a condensed version of those ones and noughts and is a number in hexadecimal. C9 is a number written with a base 16 and it equals in decimal, that is to say base 10, the number, um . . . 201.

Judge: I think I understand — has this anything to do with the kinds of things my son brings home from school as maths homework?

C.C. Yes, a great deal. These days schools teach New Mathematics in which children learn how to do addition and subtraction of numbers with different bases.

Judge: Right, so what does this 'garbage' mean?

C.C. Well, those codes give the addresses and the contents of each address. Somewhere in that pile is the validation dialogue. By carefully studying it I was able to discover that when the computer asked the validation question it looked at a particular address to find an answer to compare it with. I further investigated the matter and found that in a different part of the dump listing the contents of that address was given. When I reconverted the hexadecimal number contained in the address back into the form in which it would have been accepted by the computer, I found that it spelled out the word 'Cherry'. Thus 'Cherry' was the correct answer to the validation question.

Judge: Good, now why is it garbage?

C.C. It isn't garbage at all and I may have misled you by that statement. When a computer prints out meaningless rubbish because it has a fault we call that garbage. Occasionally, extraneous electrical signals on a communications line caused by earthing faults can produce garbage, a digital equivalent of crackles and pops on an old radio. We call these long hexadecimal printouts dumps, or dump listings, because the computer prints out, or dumps, everything relevant on the line printer.

Judge: Thank you, Professor. I suppose Mr Honey-Bunny we will have to put the 'dump' in evidence as an exhibit. Exhibit 3?

H.B. Exhibit 3 is correct, your Honour. Exhibit 1 is the original computer console log for the day in question and Exhibit 2 is the printout of the Professor's experiments. We now have, approximately, a four and a half foot thickness of computer listing paper in evidence.

Judge: Let's hope that I decide this case correctly. Their Lordships in the Court of Criminal Appeal will not take kindly to wading through reams and reams of dumps. I think we had better adjourn for lunch. The Court will resume sitting at two.

CHAPTER SIX

The Computer as a Witness III

(2.00 p.m. — Barnet Crown Court. Mr Toffee-Almond starts re-examining Professor Chocolate Chip on matters that have arisen in the cross-examination.)

T.A. Professor, my learned friend has made much of the hardware changes. Are they really relevant?

C.C. No. Think of the computer like a motor car. The central processor of the computer is the motor and the peripherals are the wheels, exhaust, etc. The tyres wear out and have to be replaced, as do brake-pads — these do not affect the working of the engine, the firing order of the cylinders.

Judge: And the operating system is like an electronic ignition system?

C.C. Exactly.[1]

[1] Professor Chocolate Chip's testimony is utter rubbish on this point. While some faults in a few peripherals can be thought of like worn tyres in a motor car, many faults can cause a feedback which can affect the operation and accuracy of the machine. An operating system is about as similar to an ignition system in a car as a gas turbine is to an egg beater. However, computer experts can be made to say strange things.

T.A. During the period between the alleged theft and your tests was the computer in daily use?

C.C. Yes, Cornet Supermarkets depended on it.

H.B. I really must object, your Honour. These matters are not within the scope of the Professor's investigation, it's hearsay.

Judge: Mr Toffee-Almond, we can't have this. These matters will no doubt be covered by later evidence.

T.A. If your Honour pleases. No further questions.

Mr Honey-Bunny asks for a ruling on the evidence of Professor Chocolate Chip. The jury is sent out and Mr Honey-Bunny asks the judge to rule that the evidence of the professor was irrelevant (but highly prejudicial) on the grounds that he did not test the computer soon enough and did not test the computer that produced the log. The judge rules that he wishes to reserve the matter to later and may direct the jury to treat the professor's evidence with some reservation. The trial continues with the jury back in court. Mr Sandwich, the data processing manager of Cornet Supermarkets, takes the stand and is sworn in.

T.A. Mr Sandwich, you are in charge of the Kamikaze computer system?

Mr S. That's right.

T.A. Would you tell the court what happened on Monday, January 27th, in the afternoon?

Mr S. Well, I'd been back from lunch for about ten minutes when I received a call from Pablo Picashew. He asked me to check the order listing against the computer log for the period between four and a quarter-to-five for the previous Friday.

T.A. And were you able to do this?

Mr S. Er, no. I produced the listing easily enough but could not find the console log.

T.A. Where should the log have been?

Mr S. The log should have been in the safe where the operator should have placed it when he finished work at six p.m. on the Saturday.

T.A. Who has the combination to the safe?

Mr S. Just the operator and me.
T.A. Where did you find the log?
Mr S. I found part of it on a desk in the supervisor's office.
T.A. What did you conclude?
Mr S. I'm afraid that I concluded that security was lax.
T.A. Mr Sandwich, do you trade on Sunday?
Mr S. No, the whole place is shut down.
T.A. Now what happened after you had found the log?
Mr S. I noted those parts of the computer runs I could, and had line printer listings made of all jobs.
T.A. And you have those with you?
Mr Sandwich gives evidence, supported by eight printouts that indicate that at 4.23 p.m. on the Friday an order was placed on the computer that resulted in the groceries being delivered to Mr Sorbet on the Saturday, charged against the stock-loss account.
T.A. Thank you. Wait there. Your witness.
H.B. Mr Sandwich, the Kamikaze computer system is a highly complex one, is it not?
Mr S. Yes, probably one of the most complex used in modern retailing.
H.B. And the logs are important?
Mr S. Very important. You see, it is a mixed batch and real-time system and the log keeps track of what is going on, particularly when a new version of the system has been brought in.
H.B. Isn't it unusual to have stock-loss as a customer account?
Mr S. It probably is, but we needed to have an account to satisfy the double-entry security requirements. Our accountants required all transactions to be recorded so that they could build in suitable audit trails. Cornet Supermarkets works on a low profit margin with a very high turnover. Stock control is the key to our success. We keep the absolute minimum of stock and the computer predicts what our sales will be each week using seasonal statistics, weather reports and new product advertising information. If we know that cheese-flavoured dog food is being promoted in the London area by television advertising,

the computer suggests that we order some unless it has statistical evidence to indicate to it that the product doesn't sell.

H.B. It certainly sounds complex.

Mr S. It is. That's why we have our own in-house software house, Spaghetti Supermarket Software. The programs to do the stock control and reordering had to be specially designed and written.

H.B. You were doing what had never been done before?

Mr S. Not exactly. We wanted to do something which had not been done but there was no innovation really involved. It meant designing a suite of programs that would do the task, and then coding them.

H.B. You followed standard industry practices?

Mr S. That's right.

H.B. *Holding up a book.* Mr Sandwich, I have here a book entitled 'Recommended Codes of Practices for the Audit of Data Processing Activities'. Have you ever seen this book?

Mr S. No.

H.B. It is an internal audit handbook published by the Institute of Internal Auditors. In designing your system you did not refer to it?

Mr S. No.

H.B. Yet you said that you followed standard industry practices.

Mr S. Yes we did. Our accountant advised us on what to do when we sent him the program specifications.

H.B. You say you designed the programs and had them coded?

Mr S. Yes.

H.B. What about testing?

Mr S. They were tested with suites of sample data and all faults that appeared were fixed.

H.B. Did new faults arise when new versions of the operating system were placed on the computer?

Mr S. Yes, and we fixed those as and when they appeared.

H.B. What about hidden errors?

Mr S. What do you mean?

H.B. Not all errors caused by changing the operating system are immediately apparent, are they?

Mr S. No, that's why the console log is so important.

H.B. Is it possible that a hidden error caused the computer to produce the record which concerns the defendant?

Mr S. It is possible, but the chances of it happening are exceedingly small. The computer would have had to have made a series of errors. First if this had been a real order taken over the telephone it would have had to have substituted a false address for that of the true recipient. Then it would have had to have substituted the account number for the stock-loss number and got round the validation routine, which is very secure. All of these are protected by fault-checking mechanisms, thus there would have to have been a rare double-fault condition in three different places at once. As I said the chances of this happening are so low as to be insignificant.

H.B. *Holding up a thick ring-bound volume.* Mr Sandwich, have you seen this book?

Mr S. Yes, it's the National Computing Centre Manual on Documentation Standards.

H.B. Do you follow it?

Mr S. Partly. We have our own internal documentation standards that are similar to those recommended.

H.B. But you don't follow the NCC standards?

Mr S. No.

H.B. And you don't follow their testing standards?

Mr S. No, we have our own.

H.B. No further questions, your Honour.

T.A. I do not need to re-examine.

Mr Sandwich leaves the stand. The trial progresses with Grapefruit Sorbet giving evidence that he was upset and did not answer the Tannoy messages but hid instead in the staff toilet. He denied the suggestion that he had used the terminal during the period but admitted he had used it for his studies on previous occasions. The prosecution starts addressing the jury when Mr Honey-Bunny asks for a two hour recess . . .

CHAPTER SEVEN
The Computer as a Witness IV

(After the two-hour recess the court is back in session.)

Judge: Yes, Mr Honey-Bunny?

H.B. May it please your Honour. I am most grateful for your indulgence in this matter. As a result of the adjournment I would like to place in evidence a British Telecom Confravision video recording which I have just made.

Judge: And what on earth is the relevance of this recording?

H.B. I have just taken evidence from a Miss Cherry Cheesecake. She was the person employed by Spaghetti Supermarket Software who designed and coded the programs, and is now working in California. Early this morning we spoke over the telephone and as a result I asked for an adjournment. I got her to go to the Los Angeles Confravision Centre where Judge Boysenberry of the California Supreme Court supervised her taking the oath. She then gave evidence in response to my questions. I recorded it all on videotape. This is the tape.

Judge: This is highly irregular.

H.B. I know your Honour, but I believe that the evidence is crucial. If my learned friend needs to cross-examine Miss Cheesecake we can do this also over a Confravision link.

Judge: In the circumstances I think we ought to see this evidence but without the jury.[1]

The jury are escorted out, a video recorder and TV set are brought in and turned on.

Cherry: I swear by Almighty God that the evidence I shall give shall be the truth, the whole truth and nothing but the truth.

H.B. *Voice on videotape.* Is your name Cherry Cheesecake and do you live at 1509 Lauren Drive, Palo Alto, California?

Cherry: Yes, that's right.

H.B. And were you the systems analyst who designed and wrote the programs for the Cornet Supermarkets' computer system?

Cherry: Yes. I did it all by myself.

H.B. Could you tell the Court what happened in December 1981 when you were writing the programs.

Cherry: You mean the visit?

H.B. That's right.

Cherry: Well, one afternoon in the middle of December, Mr Higgenbottom came to see what I was doing.

H.B. Who was Mr Higgenbottom?

Cherry: He was one of the directors of Cornet Supermarkets. He asked me a lot of questions about what my programs would do and then said, 'Look, lass, I'll come straight to the point. Cornet Supermarkets are a family concern and we have always looked after our families. My wife has always just telephoned the supermarket for groceries and they have been deliv-

[1] It is not clear how an English Court would cope with examination by video tape where the witness is outside the jurisdiction. We have taken a liberal view.

ered to her with no bill to pay or anything. How is she going to do this with your fancy new computer?'

H.B. And what did you say?

Cherry: I told him that because of the security checks built into the programs his wife would not be able to order without paying as the programs were meant to stop this happening. I said his wife would have to pay for her groceries.

H.B. And his reaction?

Cherry: He was furious. He said it was a standard directors' perk and I was to find some way of allowing his and his fellow directors' wives to continue to exercise their rights.

H.B. What did you say?

Cherry: I said I was employed to follow the specifications drawn up by Cornet Supermarkets and there was nothing in the specification mentioning directors' perks. He said he didn't care what the specifications stated and that I was to write the programs so that his wife got her free groceries or he'd see to it that I never worked as a programmer again.

H.B. So what did you do?

Cherry: Jobs were tight in 1981 and I had a mortgage. I wrote the routine he wanted. Stock-loss had an account which I knew was impersonal so I just restructured it so it was like a real customer's account. I put a note in the documentation stating that the restructuring was done for database design reasons.

H.B. What does that mean?

Cherry: Nothing, I just made it up on the spot.

H.B. Then what did you do?

Cherry: I wrote a validation routine to control entry but reversed the normal routine. I got the computer to ask what it's mother's name was.

H.B. And it accepted the answer 'Cherry' as correct?

Cherry: That's right.

H.B. Could this restructuring of yours have been an error?

Cherry: Sure, easily. We're dealing here with a mainly real-time computer system with virtual storage, paging and semi-intelligent terminals and some batch work.

What might have happened is that when one of the wives telephoned an order and had it put through using my special stock-loss routine, the computer could have made a mistake and swapped the address of the director with that of Mr Sorbet. In the batch run overnight the address could have been printed on a label for attachment to an order.

H.B. Would that require a double-fault condition?

Cherry: It might, but it needn't.

H.B. Eh?

Cherry: Well, you mentioned that Mr Sorbet had been fired and was to collect his cards on the Saturday.

H.B. Yes.

Cherry: Can you telefax me the log of batch jobs for Friday evening and overnight?

H.B. It's already with you. We call it Exhibit 6. When you've got it, could you hold it to the camera? *She does so.* That's the one.

Cherry: Right, now give me a minute. *She studies the log.* As I thought. Mr Sorbet's P45 form was being processed as a batch job about midnight on Friday — it was put in at 16.10.

H.B. So?

Cherry: Well, these forms get sent direct to the ex-employee's address when they leave employment. This means that Mr Sorbet's name and address were floating about inside the computer at the time the stock-loss order came in. Now my special routine is fairly dodgy. It isn't documented for obvious reasons and cannot therefore be checked for errors unless someone like me can isolate it. When I wrote it, the operating system in use was Version 2.1. The later systems handle files using different algorithms. It's possible that Mr Sorbet's address was swapped for that of a director's wife using the system. Her address could have been overwritten by Mr Sorbet's address. His would appear on the label to go on the package instead of hers.

H.B. Let's get this right. You wrote a secret program

having justified the existence of a stock-loss account for spurious reasons?

Cherry: No, I never had to justify my design change to anyone. I worked on my own as I said earlier and I just made up the phrase 'database design reasons' to cover me. Nobody ever questioned it because no one was employed to check my work.

H.B. O.K. You wrote this program which charges goods against stock-loss and you say that the address of the intended recipient may have got swapped with that of Mr Sorbet's which was floating around in the computer to produce his P.45?

Cherry: You got it in one, Honey-Bunny. Is that it? Can I go to work now?

H.B. I think so. We can't have you waiting there in case the prosecution want to question you.

Cherry: **O.K. but don't leave town — yes?**

H.B. If you can keep yourself available for cross-examination over the next 48 hours it would be appreciated.

Cherry: Sure thing. 'Bye.

Mr Honey-Bunny turns off the video.

Judge: A great deal of that statement is opinion.

H.B. Yes, your Honour, but we now have an alternative explanation. I submit that Miss Cheesecake's evidence demonstrates that the computer evidence cannot be relied on as any basis for a conviction.

Judge: Mr Toffee-Almond.

T.A. I do of course need to cross-examine Miss Cheesecake. However, I concede that much of the prosecution's case has been undermined if what she says is true.

H.B. There is no doubt that Mr Sorbet's cards were being processed at midnight on Friday.

Judge: I feel this case has gone on long enough. I have ruled in favour of the prosecution throughout although my personal misgivings have grown. Mr Toffee-Almond, having considered the matter I feel minded to acquit the defendant.

T.A. If that is what your Honour wishes.

The jury is called back in and directed to bring in a verdict of not guilty. Mr Grapefruit Sorbet walks free from the court and celebrates with champagne, Beluga caviar, oysters and fillet steak.

CHAPTER EIGHT
An Analysis of the Case of Grapefruit Sorbet

In this chapter we examine the implications of certain facts elicited by Mr Honey-Bunny in his questioning of the expert witness Professor Chocolate Chip and the Data Processing Manager, Mr Sandwich. A variety of dubious practices emerge all broadly revealing a poor standard of management at Cornet. We start, therefore, by describing some of the general aspects of management, as they apply to most computers that are likely to be involved in court cases. However computer technology is changing so quickly that there is a real danger when writing about it that the lead-time between manuscript and published book can render the content obsolete. Here we consider management aspects which only a relatively short time ago were the subject of numerous books and papers; the computers of that time were physically large, had a great many staff associated with them and consequently needed to be managed as any other industrial activity. Currently the media are concerned in the main with the massive growth in numbers of minicomputers and personal computers; a belief of some people is that one of the advantages of such systems is that they avoid a need for computer management. We show later that this is not necessarily so.

In Appendix A we categorise computers conveniently as mainframes, minicomputers and microcomputers. Here for a different purpose we categorise them thus:

Very large installations, value well over £1 million
Medium computer systems, value about £500 000
Small computer systems, value under £10 000

A very large installation usually requires a large number of staff. A typical list would be a director, a manager, systems analysts and programmers, document librarian, someone to disseminate information to users, a receptionist, punchroom staff, a shift supervisor, operators, maintenance engineers, tape/disk librarians, cleaners, and a security officer. With multiple shifts the numbers required of the last five types of staff increase and there can be well over fifty people involved in operations alone. It is of interest to examine some of the staff positions just listed in more detail.

A *Director* determines the overall data-processing policy in relation to the higher-level policy within the particular organisation. A large (powerful) computer installation inevitably affects all areas of activity. The Director might have a seat on the Board of Management.

A *Data Processing Manager* translates the overall policy of the director into specific attainable computer objectives. In doing so he should control the relevant staff involved in corporate computing activity. Mr Sandwich fulfils this role. In the case of a central service computer, such as the one operated by Cornet Supermarkets, a *Chief Systems Analyst* would normally maintain the software supplied with the computer, liaise on associated matters with the manufacturer's software designers and develop new software as a part of the process of improving efficiency. Whether he is subordinate to the Manager or not is an issue decided according to circumstances. If the emphasis at a given installation is on development of, say, advanced systems software *as ends in themselves* then the Chief Systems Analyst may report to the Director. If the emphasis is on the provision of a bureau service, however, as in the case of the in-house Cornet bureau, and the efforts of the Chief Systems Analyst and his staff are devoted to improving house software, then there is a case for the Chief Systems Analyst to report to the Manager. On the other hand, where an installation relies entirely on manufacturers' software packages, a Chief Systems Analyst may not be needed at all (but an arrangement of this kind is not generally desirable). Cornet Supermarkets do not appear to have a Chief Systems Analyst.

A *Supervisor* supervises the staff involved (the operators) in the running of the computer and its peripherals. On multi-shift operations, a number of operators per shift will be required, the precise number depending again on circumstances. Some computers may need only two operators, whereas one with many magnetic tape units (which require physical handling) may need a dozen. More than one supervisor is usually necessary if shift working arrangements are in force. For shift duties, staff need to be well trained and their terms of reference clearly defined.

A *Tape* and/or *Disk Librarian* maintains the supply of these items as required, keeps track of movements of media items in and out of the library and, ideally, should maintain a high standard of media cleanliness: dirty magnetic tapes can cause errors.

Data Control is an area, usually just behind a reception counter, where documents and magnetic tapes are booked in and output sorted. The same items will also be booked out and despatched. Such an area needs to be run with precision for if documents and magnetic tapes are lost the effects can be catastrophic and always expensive. Nowadays the use of remote terminals bypasses the function of a data control area unless a person at such a terminal asks for his bulk output to be printed at the centre and sent to him by van, post or messenger.

The *Disseminator of Information* looks after the mass of complex literature associated with the computer, which needs to be maintained in an orderly manner: sifted, sorted, catalogued and amended. This aspect is common to all computers, large and small, and is referred to again later.

Maintenance Engineers play a vital part in the efficient running of any installation, and operational schedules should take into account the required maintenance, work-loads being adjusted accordingly.

The question of maintenance raises an important point — whether maintenance is best done by the manufacturer under contract or by some other organisation. In the general context of maintenance there is also the need to service the air-conditioning plant regularly. Large computing installations are usually highly dependent on temperature and humidity control and will quickly develop faults if limits of temperature and humidity are exceeded.

Last, but by no means least, cleaners are necessary as most computer peripherals are sensitive to dirt and dust. Where air-conditioned environments are needed it is essential that a high standard of cleanliness is maintained. With 24-hour shift work a continuous cleaning requirement exists.

It is not until the computer falls into the category of the medium or small computer system that the management task assumes a different form. This happens because many small systems need no special working conditions such as those described above. Physically small and needing only a normal electrical power supply, they can be installed in an ordinary office environment and 'operated' by anyone who can use a keyboard and cope with the loading and unloading of a disk — similar to and no more difficult to change than a gramophone record. However the problem exists, as with all computers, that there is usually a great deal of documentation in the form of books issued by the manufacturer. These may be of simple handbook form but are more likely to be sets of volumes, one covering the equipment, another the operating system, another languages and so on. Each of these will be amended by the manufacturer periodically so there is a need to manage the insertion of new and deletion of old material. (This is rather like amending Halsbury loose leaf law reference works.) If this is not done then, for example, the software can become progressively out of date with serious consequences, as most manufacturers rely on the 'up-dates' to manuals to advise owners of errors in software and the means of correcting them — not all manufacturers are as conscientious as the Kamikaze company which advised Cornet Supermarkets by Telex of the errors found in record handling in Version 2.6. of Asthma.

In considering the final category, the smallest of the systems, it is necessary to understand the file storage concept described in Appendix A. Common to large and medium computers, they now apply to some micros. Systems with a file storage capacity of millions of characters are now available at low cost. The trend upwards in size and downwards in cost must continue and it is only a matter of time before these are available on most micros. When file systems are available, every owner of such a system will have the need to manage them to avoid administrative chaos.

Thus the whole range of computers from the largest to the smallest already have or will soon have a need for management of one form or another. Mr Sandwich as the operations manager of a large computer installation is responsible for running the entire installation in an efficient manner and maintaining performance. He did not do this very well. Had he been a professional member of either the Institute of Data Processing Management or the British Computer Society, adhered to their Codes of Conduct and Practice and been familiar with, say, the contents of 'Guidelines for Computing Management' published by the National Computing Centre, then Mr Grapefruit Sorbet may never have had to be arraigned. However Mr Sandwich did not achieve such standards, for several deficiencies were revealed under cross-examination. For example, sections of the console log were missing. No one knew precisely what version of the operating system was running at specific times, and the significance of the Telex from the Kamikaze company had clearly not been appreciated. Indeed from the transcript of the Court proceedings it would seem that Mr Honey-Bunny had more up-to-date information on that issue than either Professor Chocolate Chip or Mr Sandwich. Also, coffee had been taken into the computer room and spilled on equipment.

A particularly damning incident, was the lack of software control procedures, which allowed Cherry Cheesecake not only to design, write and develop the special software for the Cornet Supermarkets' order and stock handling routines, but to bring it to the state of a fully operational system with no direct supervision by senior management of either Cornet Supermarkets or Spaghetti Software. Mr Honey-Bunny achieved his aim, by getting Cherry Cheesecake to reveal the existence of her private modification. He could have gone on to reveal possible deficiencies in the planning and control of the programming activity as a whole. For example, if in-house documentation standards had been rigorously applied with independent vetting then it is highly unlikely that Cherry's directors' perk modification would have been successfully installed.

Professor Chocolate Chip obtained the master password from Mr Sandwich with apparent ease . This was a quite flagrant breach of security. Mr Sandwich should have supplied the master listing and not allowed the Professor himself to have access to the system.

Although Mr Honey-Bunny succeeded in proving Grapefruit Sorbet innocent, Sorbet's admitted excursions into the terminal room in order to use a terminal for his homework were highly incriminating. They revealed a further serious weakness in the security arrangements in force at Cornet Supermarkets. The Asthma operating system had a 'password' facility which meant that each legitimate user of a VDU connected to the Kamikaze computer system could be allocated a password which he or she will need to type in at the VDU keyboard before Cherry's validation routine was entered. However there was an administrative task involved in setting up a password system. Mr Sandwich either did not set up, or failed to monitor, the control procedures necessary to make the password system an effective means of controlling access. As a result he had a highly vulnerable computer system. Since Grapefruit Sorbet was a shelf-filler with no need to enter the terminal room he would not have been issued with a password — yet he must have acquired knowledge of one for he is known to have successfully 'logged in' and used the computer for his own purposes. Furthermore he must have acquired knowledge of the validation 'dialogue'.

We draw attention in Chapter 2 to some of the error-checking mechanisms that are incorporated into computers and their peripherals. These, however, cannot help where someone like Grapefruit Sorbet has successfully gained illegal access. So far as the Kamikaze system is concerned Sorbet would be regarded as legitimate for he had a password and knew the correct answer to the validation question. As he had found a means of penetrating the file-store his work would be 'hidden from view' because of the difficult task faced by central management if they are required to know the contents of a user's files.

There are methods of monitoring the work run on computers. Some may be inherent in the operating system and these will ensure that a brief record of all 'jobs' is maintained on, say, the console log if such a device exists, or, alternatively, on a disk file which will maintain a record of all activity on an operator's VDU.

It may be difficult however to detect relatively minor tasks such as the elementary homework of Mr Sorbet or the activation of Cherry Cheesecake's perks routine. For such detection tasks it is necessary to incorporate audit trails whose purpose is to aid examination of the operation of controls which have been incorporated. There are three main categories of audit coverage; the one of relevance here applies at the file interrogation levels. Enquiry programs should exist to test files and, by random selection at random times, to extract and analyse data for examination.

Grapefruit Sorbet gained access to the terminal room and thence access to the Kamikaze. In doing so he breached the software security safeguards. He could, however, have been prevented from gaining access to the room itself by means of hardware security features. A lock on the door of the terminal room controlled by a key issued only to authorised personnel would have formed an effective first barrier. Thereafter each terminal could have been of the type fitted with a lock which prevents the terminal being switched on and operated until the correct key is inserted.

As security procedures cost money to implement and enforce, senior management must determine the degree of exposure to illegal access and balance this against the cost of successful penetration. Mr Sorbet obtained (albeit innocently) goods to the value of approximately £25. A determined and successful penetration could easily have generated a complete van-load of orders worth many hundreds of pounds. Without any need to resort to guns, knives and violence quite obviously computer shoplifting is entering a different world. We deal briefly with computer crime in Appendix B.

CHAPTER NINE
A Brief for the Future

The object of this final chapter is to suggest ways in which the parties in cases involving computer evidence can present the relevant facts to the court and get the court to attach the correct weight to the said evidence. Many matters are non-contentious and a considerable amount of time can be saved in the courtroom if the issues can be clearly defined at an early stage.

Computer evidence can only be admissible if it is reliable. The bare statement by a data processing manager that the computer was working properly is a statement of opinion that must be elaborated upon. However, because the Civil Evidence Act 1968 used a particular form of words and a similar form of words has been suggested by the Criminal Law Revision Committee (Cmnd. 4991 paragraph 259, page 150) for inclusion in a future criminal evidence act that specifically deals with computers, computer personnel tend to make depositions or swear affidavits that read something like the draft below:

1. I, Sidney Orville Sandwich, make oath and say as follows: I

am the manager of the Cornet Supermarkets Computer Centre at Hendon, London. I occupy a responsible position in relation to the management of that centre and I make this statement pursuant to Section 1 of the Criminal Evidence Act 1965.

2. There is now produced and shown to me a document marked S.O.S.1 which is a printout showing entries in the computerised order book of Cornet Supermarkets of orders taken on Friday, 25th January 1983.
3. I confirm from records in the possession of the Cornet Supermarket's Computer Centre that the printout was produced during the period over which the computer was used regularly to store or process information for business purposes regularly carried on over that period.
4. I confirm from those records that over the said period there was regularly supplied to the computer in the ordinary course of those activities, information of the kind contained in the printout, or of the kind from which the information so contained is derived.
5. I confirm that throughout the material part of the said period the computer was operating properly, and that the information contained in the printout reproduces or is derived from information supplied to the computer in the ordinary course of the business of Cornet Supermarkets.

Statements of this kind are not helpful to the court or to Counsel. If in our case, Mr Honey-Bunny had only had the benefit of an affidavit of this kind he would have been faced with a stark choice. On the one hand he could have cross-examined Mr Sandwich for several days requesting adjournments to consider each of the matters revealed — the make of computer, the working environment, the level of security, the testing and documentation standards etc. This would have led to a case that might well have cost the public purse via Legal Aid many tens of thousands of pounds if the judge had allowed it. On the other hand if he had permitted the deposition to be put in without calling the data processing manager he would have allowed Mr Sorbet to be convicted.

In our view a new form of affidavit or deposition should be used to produce computer evidence in both criminal and civil cases so that the question of reliability of computer evidence can be adequately argued in court. We suggest that to do this the person in charge of the computer system who, naturally, wishes the evidence to be relied upon should highlight the key features of the system that go to the issue of reliability. We believe this could be done by use of an affidavit or deposition in seven parts — The Seven Statements.

The Seven Statements

Statement One should deal with the qualifications and experience of the person in charge of the computer system. This is to establish that he is capable of swearing such a document.

Statement Two should consist of a description of the computer system with reference to each of the components in the system by brand and model number, e.g. a Kamikaze DDB7 with the Asthma 2.6 operating system running custom written payroll programs. Statement Three, a long statement, should deal with the quality of the individual components by reference to the development time involved in their creation. For example reference could be made here to any technical literature or manuals which were used, giving the number of man hours involved in their original development. Manufacturers of quality products would gladly assist in producing technical evidence of this kind. Statement Four should deal with the testing and documentation standards applied to any custom written software. If the software had been bought-in, the software house, if reputable, should be willing to provide information on its testing and documentation standards.

Statement Five should deal with the procedures for logging updates to the software and the qualifications of the subordinate staff involved in the computer system.

Statement Six should deal with the physical and electronic security features of the installation.

Finally, Statement Seven should indicate how the particular computer printout came into existence and what it purports to show. In this section the person in charge can say that no faults manifested themselves during the material time which would indicate to him that the computer evidence could not be relied upon.

In a criminal case a deposition made by the person in charge of the computer system containing the Seven Statements would greatly assist both counsel and the judge in determining the reliability of the computer system and hence whether the evidence could be put before a jury. A document containing the Seven Statements would be extremely lengthy but much of it could and, we believe, should, be prepared by an organisation using computers prior to any incident requiring the organisation to go to law or to assist in a prosecution. The first six of the Seven Statements could be kept in draft form on file. It would then be a simple and inexpensive process finally to add the Seventh Statement and engross the document attaching any relevant computer printouts to it as exhibits.

Readers may now have realised that Mr Honey-Bunny in his brief was actually presented with a deposition containing the Seven Statements; there is no way that a busy criminal barrister could have cross-examined the computer expert with such devastating effect were he not assisted by a technical deposition of the kind outlined. It is in the interest of justice for the courts to require that in all cases when evidence from a computer is tendered, an affidavit or deposition containing the Seven Statements is produced with the said evidence.

Pre-trial Proceedings

It is common practice for lawyers to be presented with the papers in a case they are to argue either the night before the trial or a few minutes before the trial. For a case involving computer evidence this is clearly in nobody's real interest. It is felt by the authors that in criminal cases, in the same way that the accused has to give an alibi warning to the prosecution, if either side wishes to rely on computer evidence that party must give notice and particulars of the evidence either at the committal proceedings or within seven days thereafter. Unless and until a Practice Note to this effect is issued the disadvantaged party should be given a favourable hearing when requesting an adjournment to study and digest computer evidence. In civil cases where a dispute arose concerning the reliability of the computer evidence many of the matters could be disposed of by proper use of interrogatories, which would save both time in the courtroom and cost.

The Lawyer in the Courtroom

While it is hoped that the lawyer will only have to rely upon competent and independent experts to assist him in presenting or rebutting computer evidence, it will often be the case that no such person can be found, or that Legal Aid funds do not extend to cover the cost of such highly qualified people. In such circumstances the lawyer has no alternative but to attempt to do the expert's job. In this difficult situation some rules of thumb may assist:

1. Most computers have an operating system (see Appendix A). These are in a constant state of development with new versions frequently being released. It can be said that an operating system which has been under continuous development for several years is less likely to have latent errors than an operating system that is relatively new.
2. Similarly, hidden faults in computer hardware are more likely to be present in newly developed components (16-bit microprocessors and 64K memory chips are examples of new components). The hobby computer market may be supplied with faulty chips or chips of a lower quality than would otherwise be acceptable. Thus any computer made from these faulty components would be more prone to production of errors.
3. Computers connected together in a network are more likely to produce undetected errors than a computer system of equivalent power based around a central mainframe. This is because networking is a newer technology and the associated operating systems are frequently still in an experimental stage of development and the professional qualifications of the staff involved may not be uniform throughout the network. Compared with centralised facilities the quality of the working environment for the computers may be lower throughout the network and the physical security lower because of the increase in the number of locations where global alterations to the database can be made. However, the fusion of digital telephone technology with computer technology should, over the next few years, greatly reduce errors. Digital telephone systems use microprocessors linked together in a network while

present-day computers systems are still based round a single central processor. The problems of staff and security are likely nevertheless to remain.

4. A computer program is less likely to contain latent errors when the algorithm from which it was coded has been designed carefully, and within a disciplined environment. There are a variety of different techniques covered by the terms 'software engineering' and 'structured programming'. Many books have been written to assist users in producing good designs and the National Computing Centre is a mine of information. The software designer will frequently flowchart the logical sequence he wishes the program to follow and special flowcharting languages are available to assist him in ensuring that no logic errors are present in the design. Some organisations that are very concerned about the quality of their designs impose strict rules on how a designer may flowchart. The constraints vary, but the object is the same — to stop the flowchart resembling a tangled web and instead force the designer to be rigorous in his approach.

5. At a level of detail, programs that are written using nested loop structures rather than 'go to' statements indicate that the program has probably been written with more rigorous quality control. Frequent comment statements indicating what each part of the program is meant to be doing are also indications of quality. A program that is made up of individually tested modules is often better than an integrated program doing the equivalent task.

The Computer Professional in the Courtroom

Nothing is worse than the pedantic technician who relapses into jargon when asked to justify an opinion. Under cross-examination an honest man can be made to look a liar if he does not carefully consider his words. Any computer professional must remember that if a lawyer can show in open court that he does not know what he is talking about his career prospects are very likely wrecked. Professor Chocolate Chip, an honest but myopic witness, may be unable to find good work once Mr Sorbet's case is reported in the computer press. The guiding rule is therefore not to express an opinion that you cannot support by reference to known facts.

Although computer professionals and lawyers speak different languages they both live in a society where justice according to law is justifiably revered. They will ensure its continued pinnacle position only if they work together in the development of computer evidence law. Very soon, because of the growing use of computers, almost every litigious matter will involve computer evidence. Computer personnel must take the responsibility that has been thrust upon them and behave in a professional manner. Lawyers must embark on the harder task of learning how to present and defend cases involving computer evidence. The law, which is designed to protect the weak against the strong, must protect those who do not understand computers from those who do. Only if lawyers are in the latter class can law be a synonym for justice.

APPENDIX A
Some Computer Basics

A number of technical terms (operating system, files, application program, real-time clock, etc.) are used in the book particularly in the chapters concerned with cross-examination. This appendix explains in elementary terms what the lawyers and witnesses are talking about. Readers who wish to pursue matters further are referred to Appendix C. We wish to point out, however, that it is not necessary to understand any of the following before *using* a computer.

How Computers Work

A computer consists of four hardware components: an input/output unit, a control unit, a memory unit and an arithmetic unit. In principle, the data is read-in by the input unit and routed by the control unit to the memory unit. The arithmetic unit carries out logical processes such as sorting, comparing and selecting as well as arithmetical operations such as addition and subtraction. After a number of these processes have been carried out the results are placed in the memory unit by the control unit and the new information subsequently made available by the output unit.

Additional hardware, refinements on the basic concept, consist of 'backing memory' which, in effect, extends the size of the main memory, and 'registers', which are transient memories located in other units and which hold information, under instruction, only during the course of a calculation or logical process.

The computer (hardware) has to be instructed to carry out each and every step. Some of these instructions relate to means by which the computer functions once it has started a computation (like sending output to a printer), and can be regarded as control instructions. The others will instruct the computer to carry out a specific task such as performing an income tax calculation.

All the above hardware elements can be grouped more meaningfully: the control unit, memory unit and arithmetic unit (each with its registers) form the central processor unit (CPU). Backing memory remains distinct while the input/output unit and associated registers exist as separate component parts known as the 'peripherals' — magnetic tape units, punched card readers, printers, visual display units, etc. The list of instructions to tell the computer to perform a task (typically an income tax calculation) is called the application program (the spelling with one 'm' conforms with the British Standard and avoids confusion with programme of work). The numbers used in the calculation are referred to as the data.

The control instructions already referred to would be resident in the computer before the application program is read-in. These control instructions are usually covered by the term 'operating system' although certain control functions are performed by the hardware and are not therefore, strictly speaking, a part of the software operating system. For present purposes however the term operating system software will be taken to include all control functions.

Because we are concerned here with errors that can be made by a computer, it is necessary to deal with that aspect of digital computers, binary notation, which is the most difficult to understand for those people who have no knowledge of coding techniques and logical algebra. Fully to comprehend the digital computer and how it works needs a knowledge of these, and electronics. Nevertheless an elementary comprehension certainly sufficient for the purposes of this book, can be gained by consideration of a few basic principles.

Reference is made in Chapter 1 to the fact that a digital computer can deal only with one of two states. More accurately, the elementary component out of which each of the basic units is made can be only in one of two states. Thus one considers such a component (or element) as being open or closed, on or off, set or not set, and so on. A formal logic based on this principle was developed by George Boole in the nineteenth century using the symbols 0 and 1; one of the first uses of 'Boolean algebra' was in the derivation of actuarial tables long before digital computers existed. Binary notation is the term used nowadays to describe such a system. Errors arise when a state which should be 0 is 1 and vice versa. Without extensive safeguards, it is only too easy for this to happen.

It so happens that the basic electronic element, out of which computers are made and which can reside in one of two states is a simple one while an electronic element capable of residing in more than one state is complex. Computers based on such elements have been designed and built but for all practical purposes the happy coincidence that Boolean (or binary) logic is easily and cheaply translated into electronic components has established the binary principle of digital computers. Looked at another way, the binary system is a method of coding. Decimal numbers can be coded in binary, as can the letters of the alphabet and other characters such as brackets and asterisks.

This, in effect, is what happens in certain input/output units of a computer system. It also takes place in the preparatory stages external to the computer where, say, cards are punched to form input documents. The binary principle follows all the way through — a hole or no hole is punched or not punched in a given location on a card or section of paper tape; an electronic signal or no signal results from there being a hole or no hole in the paper medium; a binary digit (bit) is then set (at 1) or not set (0) in a register; a memory location is then filled (1) or not filled (0); an area of magnetic tape is magnetised in one direction (1) or the other (0). (As mentioned earlier, errors exist when a given state is intended to be 1 but is, in fact 0. It is such an event which causes, say, overtime to be subtracted instead of added in a payroll calculation.)

The above, however, oversimplifies the computational process in suggesting that the coding is uniform throughout. This is not so, for while the binary system applies throughout, a different code is used after the input unit.

To explain this we need to recall that human beings understand the spoken word and can write words and read each other's words (assuming a common language). By and large a computer is insensitive to such forms of communication (the source code) so to communicate with a computer, instructions in conventional human notation have first to be coded (using the binary system) into a form that the appropriate input peripheral can handle. A further stage is then necessary to convert them into a form (the object code) which the computer proper can handle efficiently. With a device such as a visual display unit (VDU), which consists of a small television screen and a typewriter keyboard, coding and decoding are largely carried out within the unit itself, so that immediately human-readable characters are typed in and the results displayed similarly on the screen.

What follows is a brief description of the way in which binary coding is effected at the source code level.

In the conventional (or Arabic) numbering system the shape of the symbol conveys information. For example from the shape '6' we understand it to mean 'six', the shape '5' to mean 'five', and so on. In the binary system only two symbols, 0 and 1 are used. One looks instead for a position of the 0s and 1s in a 'table' of one row usually read from right to left. One such table, often known as a byte, has eight positions as follows:

0	0	0	0	0	1	1	0

Position 8   Position 1

As the table is conceptual in nature, unless there is a specific reason for drawing it it is usual to leave out the lines so the above example would normally be written:

00000110

We can add to the table the equivalent in decimal numbers against the corresponding bit position:

```
          2⁶   2⁴   2²   2⁰
          /    /    /    /
      0  0  0  0  0  1  1  0
     /      \     \     \
   2⁷        2⁵    2³    2¹
```

The positional *values* in the above table are given for clarification purposes only. They are not normally shown.

Bearing in mind that, here, binary symbol 0 is taken to be decimal number zero (which can be read as meaning 'not present') the last table can be used to illustrate coding:

> In the first position (the first on the right) a one is not present (because $0 \times 2^0 = 0$)
> In the second position two is present (because $1 \times 2^1 = 2$)
> In the third position four is present (because $1 \times 2^2 = 4$)
> In the fourth position eight is not present (because $0 \times 2^3 = 0$) and so on.

'Decoding' the byte gives:

> $0 + 0 + 0 + 0 + 0 + 4 + 2 + 0$ and 4 plus 2 equals 6.

The decimal numbers from 0 to 12 can be expressed as 'patterns' in tabular byte form as follows:

Decimal number	Binary pattern
0	00000000
1	00000001
2	00000010
3	00000011
4	00000100
5	00000101
6	00000110
7	00000111
8	00001000

Decimal number	Binary pattern
9	00001001
10	00001010
11	00001011
12	00001100

In a computer a set of electronic components will correspond and hold states representing the positions in the table, the components forming, say, an 8-position electronic 'register'. Manipulation is possible because each is capable of being switched to a conducting (1) or non-conducting (0) state, so changing the pattern in a given position in the table.

While there is no limit in theory to the number of bits in a byte, in practice it is usually limited to eight (as shown in the examples) for input/output stages and devices. In some computers bytes can, collectively, become 'words' which have a certain length. For example a minicomputer might have a word length of 32 bits (four 8-bit bytes) and a larger computer a word length of 64 bits. Generally speaking the longer the word length the more powerful the computer. An example of a 16-bit word is:

0100110010011011

The size of a computer memory is often given in terms of words, e.g. 512,000 words (written usually as 512K words where K is loosely taken to be 1000, but is actually 1024).

In Chapter 5 Professor Chocolate Chip made reference to hexadecimal notation. Expressed on paper, binary representation can be very long and unwieldy. For this reason it is easier for those people who are investigating faults in a computer, and have to examine a set of binary symbols, if they are expressed in a more condensed manner. To achieve this the 'pure' binary is converted to 'hexadecimal' form. However, this involves no major change because each group of four digits in binary corresponds to a single digit in hexadecimal (since 2^4 equals 16). Thus our 16-bit word:

0100110010011011

can be broken down into four sections:

0100 1100 1001 1011

Each of these can be converted into a single hexadecimal digit.

However, because there is no single symbol or sign that we can use for numbers like eleven or twelve, letters of the alphabet are used in their place. Thus:

Decimal number	Hexadecimal symbol
0	0
1	1
etc	etc
8	8
9	9
10	A
11	B
12	C
13	D
14	E
15	F

Our 16-bit word is:

4 C 9 B in hexadecimal

The patterns representing 4 and 9 can be verified from the table of decimal numbers and binary equivalents while the above table shows that C is representative of decimal 12 which is 1100 in binary.

Sometimes conversions are made to a base of eight, which is called octal and in which each digit corresponds to a group of three binary digits instead of four, because two cubed is eight.

When a computer is required to, say, multiply two numbers, it does it by manipulation of binary:

Binary Patterns	Corresponds to	Decimal Numbers
010	$(0 \times 4) + (1 \times 2) + (0 \times 1) =$	2
$\times$011	$(0 \times 4) + (1 \times 2) + (1 \times 1) =$	$\times$3
010		
100		
110	$(1 \times 4) + (1 \times 2) + (0 \times 1) =$	6

As already indicated, non-numeric characters can also be

coded and manipulated in binary. The following is an example of the ASCII code for computer peripherals:

Character	Pattern	Character	Pattern
A	11000001	)	10101001
B	11000010	#	10100011
C	11000011	/	10101111
D	11000100	*	10101010
E	11000101	(	10101000
F	11000110	%	10100101

that is, a character is represented by its position in an alphabet. An 'A' will be changed to, say, an 'F' by a programmed 'instruction' and a consequent computer function which changes 11000001 to 11000110.

The logic elements out of which computers are made can be expressed in binary before being 'built'. Once existing as hardware, they carry out the functions of which a given computer is capable. There are three forms of logical element out of which other elements can be made. The first element is called an inverter. It has one input and one output:

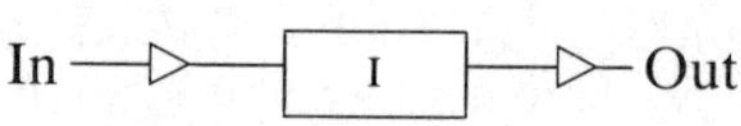

The relationship between input and output is expressed in a binary truth table:

Input	Output
0	1
1	0

which means that when the input is 0 the output is 1, and vice versa. These are the only states in which an inverter can reside.

The next element is the '2-input AND gate' shown thus:

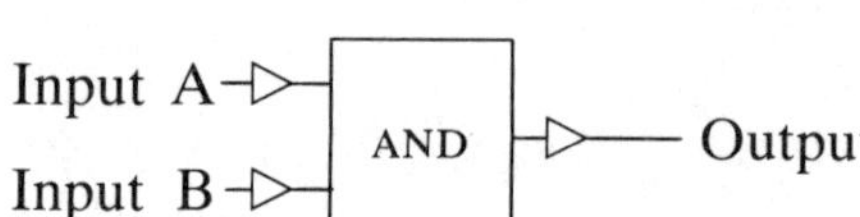

The truth table is:

Input A	Input B	Output
0	0	0
0	1	0
1	0	0
1	1	1

This shows that the output is 1 only when the two inputs are 1. An AND gate can have more than two inputs. In this case the output is 1 only if *all* the inputs are 1s.

The third element is the OR gate:

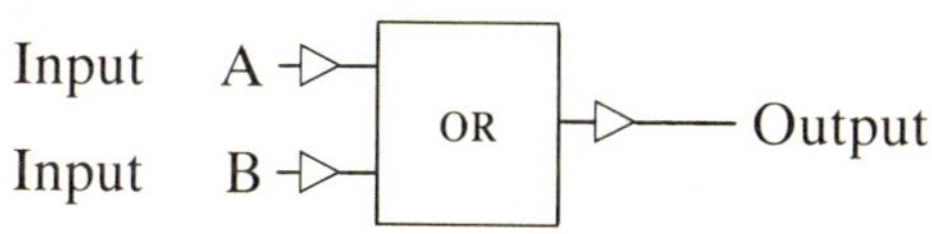

Input A	Input B	Output
0	0	0
1	0	1
0	1	1
1	1	1

The output is 1 when either (or both) of the inputs is 1. An OR gate can have more than two inputs. In this case the output is 1 if any of the inputs is a 1.

Hardware units of a computer are made up of hundreds and thousands of gates and inverters mounted on boards connected by intricate wiring. The full implications of large-scale integration (LSI) are brought home when it is realised that many thousands of gates can be formed on a single piece of silicon (the chip) about $\frac{1}{8} \times \frac{1}{8}$ inch.

It is sufficient to end this brief description by pointing out that all of the elements described can be switched on or off, opened or closed, set or unset usually synchronised, in fractions of a second by a series of control signals originating within a computer's own time clock. All together they can perform millions of logical operations while, for example, a person at a VDU keyboard is moving a finger from one key to the next!

To return now to coding. Conversion from the source code to the object code takes place after the immediate reading-in process, and is under the control of the computer itself. It is carried out by a special type of program, one example of which is a 'compiler'. Each language has its own compiler, thus COBOL compiler, BASIC compiler, FORTRAN compiler etc.

The above can be considered in a structured sequence:

Stage 1: Devising the algorithm.
The person who wishes to use a computer (called, say, a programmer or 'user') prescribes a set of rules for the solution of his problems in a finite number of steps. This is called an 'algorithm', which the user will understand but which will mean nothing to the computer and which cannot be communicated to it at this stage.
Stage 2: Coding
The user will transcribe the algorithm into a program using the rules of a given language which again the user understands but which will still not be in a form which can be understood by the computer.
Stage 3: Compiling.
The computer by the use of a compiler will convert the program in source code (obtained from the input device) to object code, which it now can understand.
Stage 4: Executing.
The program will then be 'executed'; that is, run to perform the task (say an income tax calculation) but it will also need 'data', in this case numbers representing someone's income and characters relating to his tax code.

To explain the last sentence of Stage 4 we need to understand that a program actually consists of two parts — 'program' and 'data'. Taking 'program' first, this is the set of instructions defining the task which often starts by being written in English (Stage 1 above). The following program is really too simple to qualify for the term algorithm but it illustrates how the task can be expressed in formal terms:

Take a number from location A
Take a number from location B
Add A to B
Put the result in Location C

This simple program needs two numbers, one ready in location A of the memory, the other ready in location B. After the program has been compiled for execution purposes (that is, running the program) the computer will fetch the two numbers held in A and B, add them together and send the result back to location C. The two numbers held in A and B are the 'data' needed by the 'program'.

What makes the computer powerful is its ability to perform 'conditional' operations. For example, the simple program above could be extended so that after, say, the numbers held in A and B are added, the result could be compared, say, with a previously computed number held in another memory location. The computer can be instructed (programmed) to do then one of three things depending on whether the comparison shows that the contents of A and B added together are equal to, greater or less than the third number.

The above example of a program is a single entity; most modern computers of any size can run a number of programs simultaneously, all of them a good deal more complicated than the example and all with considerable quantities of data. This ability to run a number of programs simultaneously is known as multiprogramming. In a lot of cases the individuals (users) using the computer may well be miles away from each other with the computer being connected to their remote VDUs via a communication system. These users will not generally be aware of each other's existence. Such a method of use is known as 'remote access time-sharing'. A more complex system is where several computers, remote from each other, are connected together in, say, a ring. Each will have connected to it VDUs from which a user can access any computer in the ring. Alternatively, the remote computers can be connected to a large central computer, so forming a 'star' configuration. The terms 'network' and 'distributed computing' are loosely applied to both.

The imaginary Kamikaze computer system used by Cornet Supermarkets is a centralised mainframe system providing a service to the supermarket chain. A network of minicomputers, or possibly a hybrid network of mini- and microcomputers, could, broadly, perform a similar function. It is of interest therefore to examine the differences between the different types of machine. Before doing so we feel it necessary to describe briefly the 'file' concept — a term now widely used in computing and by Professor Chocolate Chip. (In computer terms a file is a set of related records treated as a unit.) Most readers will be familiar with the manilla file, the filing cabinet and the registry where cabinets hold files just as a library holds books. Each file will have a title and often a reference number, and be stored in cabinets in a certain sequence. A particular file can be located by the number, and the contents checked by reference to the title. Such a file can be 'opened' so that the contents can be read, worked on and added to.

Many computers have a file store organised in a similar way though the files consist of magnetic patterns on, say, the magnetisable surface of disks. Each file will have some form of reference enabling it to be quickly located and the contents made available at, say, a terminal. A new file can be opened, an old one deleted; the contents can be read, amended, appended to, deleted, and so on, before being returned to the file store. Conversion to and from human-readable form takes place somewhere in the computer system between the file store and the input/output device.

Just as a file registry has to be organised if it is to be efficient, so have the files in a computer system. One way of doing this is to have a directory, which is an organised list of all files in that system. Directories and files may also need protection. There are many ways of accomplishing this, such as the 'password' system. For convenience, the reader can imagine a safe with a combination lock. The person who knows the combination (password) can open it to find, inside, a box itself bearing another combination lock. Only if the person knows that combination as well can he open the box and get at the contents. Computer directories and files can be protected in this manner to a considerable depth, that is boxes within boxes within boxes each requiring the use of a unique password to access the next level down.

A computer of even modest size will have thousands of files. As a file system is a part of the particular operating system (see later in this appendix) they represent several years of development so are only recently available with microcomputers. Micro filing systems are cheap; just over £1000 will buy a system with a storage capacity of millions of characters.

We can now return to the discussion of the different types of computer.

Mainframe Computers

Generally, these will usually either provide a bureau service to a large number of users or allow application programs to be run that demand considerable resources because they are very large or complex — such as a weather-forecasting program or one simulating oil resources. However, mainframe machines can no longer be regarded as necessarily physically large (relative to minicomputers) because the advances in the techniques of large-scale integration (LSI) have made it possible to reduce greatly their physical size. Probably the only worthwhile distinction left between mainframes and the larger minicomputers is one of cost. A reasonable cross-over point from mini to mainframe is where a given computer complex costs more than £1M, will have a comprehensive operating system, use 24-bit words and upwards, and probably support hundreds of terminals connected to the computer but situated possibly miles away. There will be a wide range of supporting software, a full range of peripherals such as printers and graph plotters. In general a special building, air-conditioning, power supplies and many support staff will bc rcquircd.

Minicomputers

A minicomputer-based complex may consist of a processor, main memory, backing store and peripherals, such as a printer and card-reader. At one time word lengths were 16 bits. Nowadays 32-bit machines are common place. A minicomputer system can conveniently be regarded as being limited by size, for example when a particular configuration can no longer function in a normal office environment.

It has been claimed that minicomputers can perform equivalent roles (in terms of total task capacity) to mainframe machines. In the single case this may be true, but in an organisation the use of many minicomputers may bring problems such as the difficulty of achieving a commonality of media and documentation standards. As already mentioned a number of minicomputers can be connected by a network to resemble a large system, but to accomplish this, at least proven network software is necessary.

Microcomputers

The microcomputer is a product of large-scale integration (LSI) where elements such as the complete processor can be 'packaged in a small element about 1 × 0.5 × 0.125 inches'. The original microprocessors were of 4-bit word length, but are now obtainable in 16-bit form. In general the normal peripherals have to be added and the complete system is then quite large and, in some cases, expensive.

Components such as additional memory can be bought cheaply, and quite powerful microcomputers can be assembled, though the problems of programming on any large scale as with any computer can be time-consuming and formidable. Most computer peripherals and terminals now incorporate microprocessors as custom-designed components, hence giving rise to the term 'intelligent terminal'.

Operating Systems for Mainframes and Minis

With many time-sharing users and large numbers of remote terminals the role of the operating system is an important one. In the ideal case, hardware and system software will have been designed to complement one another. The ultimate efficiency, security, reliability and resilience of a computer are governed by the way its operating system and hardware interact.

Within this general context, in terms of its ability to do work, a computer consists of 'resources'; users have to compete for use of the units already mentioned such as the central processor, the memory and the peripheral devices. Often, possibly for reasons of economy for example, programs and data may need to be shared by a group of users so some control of this type of common use is necessary. Conversely, other users may want to keep their programs and data entirely private yet available to themselves whenever they wish to use them. This means the operating system has to recognise and distinguish between group and individual owners and to hold their files (programs and data) somewhere in the system for weeks or months as appropriate and yet have them available, when so instructed, in a matter of minutes.

In all the above cases, and particularly where simultaneous running is possible, there is clearly a need for complex protection procedures. Many installations need to charge for the provision of such services so the ability to account accurately for their use is a necessity. An operating system then has to be comprehensive yet easy to use and unobtrusive so far as the user is concerned. As it has to be able to resolve conflicts arising from simultaneous requests for the same resource, a policy is necessary and also a means of enforcement: both must be able to withstand the attacks of 'hostile' user programs. The operating system should be able to record details, at small discrete intervals of time, of its performance and efficiency against chosen criteria.

APPENDIX B
Computer Crime — A Legal Catch-22?

The English Adversary System of Justice allows technical legal arguments. In the sphere of computer crime many such arguments can arise as the statutory definitions of words such as 'document', 'criminal damage', and 'property' were drafted without computers in mind. There is concern about 'burglary by telephone' whereby the thief using the telephone system makes unauthorised use of a computer or extracts valuable information from a databank. The scope for such activities is increased by the movement towards computer networks. Alteration or damage to goods belonging to another is prosecuted normally under the Criminal Damage Act 1977 and serious doubts exist as to whether unauthorised access to a computer from a remote terminal causing damage to the intangible information stored in the computer is prosecutable under the Act.

A possible argument that could totally wreck any prosecutions for computer fraud is a Catch-22 type argument. We have chosen as an example a variation on our Grapefruit Sorbet case. Suppose Cornet Supermarkets' auditors suddenly discovered that the number of stock-losses had gone up threefold, and that the losses commenced two months after the employment of a new systems programmer with access to the entire system and without supervision. On further investigation the programs are found to contain a 'patch' — that is to say an unauthorised piece of software such as the special routine created by Miss Cherry Cheesecake. If the programmer was well advised legally and made no admissions, the company would encounter the following problem:

> All the evidence against the programmer emanates from the computer.
> Computer evidence is only admissible when the computer is working properly.
> A computer is not working properly when its programs are 'patched' illegally.
> Therefore there is no admissible evidence against the programmer.

When a business depends on the computer for keeping the records and the computer is or has been subverted by criminals the evidence from the computer is unreliable. In any case information is stored in an ephemeral manner inside the computer and can be altered very easily and quickly. Most of the known case studies of computer crimes have been carried out by Parker *et al.*[1], who have files of over 800 specific cases. There are also many stories in circulation and although some may well be apocryphal, they are plausible, and none would be impossible to achieve by someone who has a knowledge of computers and computer systems and the opportunity to use that knowledge.

One of the biggest computer frauds on record occurred in the US insurance industry. The fraud was carried out by computer specialists employed by the company who devised a way of creating 'lives' by inventing data about them and inputting these to the computer system in standard insurance format. The lives and future income from the associated premiums were then sold to reinsurance companies for cash. 'People' were later given a death pattern at suitable intervals of time to 'balance the books'.

A further story concerns a bank system analyst who noticed that transactions commonly involved many dollars and a few cents. He devised a 'hidden' software routine, which rounded down such accounts to the nearest dollar, the few cents being transferred to an account of his own created for the purpose. It is claimed that he quickly accumulated over $1M.

A third story illustrates another approach: a bank introduced personal character-coded paying-in slips, using magnetic ink invisible to the eye. Someone to whom a book of slips had been issued, and who knew of the use of the characters, separated the slips and distributed them amongst public trays in branches of the bank. Customers filled them in, signed them and handed them over the counter. The computer system, however, ignored the real depositor's signature and put the money in the account indicated by the magnetic code. Norman[(2)] has many more of these stories.

The insurance fraud was eventually detected by conventional audit; the next two would have been more difficult to detect. Computer frauds have demonstrated clearly that many of the controls (against collusion, for example) that existed in manual systems were abandoned in the conversion to computer systems. Instead of responsibility being shared by two or more people, as in manual systems, in a computer system the responsibility may well be invested in one programmer who may not only control accounts payable, purchase orders and approvals for payment, but may also carry responsibility (on grounds of economy) for devising the computer audit program. Recall that Cherry Cheesecake was unsupervised and, on her own admission, did not have to justify the insertion of a patch. The temptation to incorporate hidden changes to the program to render it unable to detect certain transactions is a real one. Unless there is professional discipline in system design and programming, records of changes to software will not be maintained so, again, there may be no obvious clue for a human auditor.

In addition to ensuring that joint responsibility is a requirement, an audit trail is necessary that monitors internally at specific software levels what can be regarded as targets. For example, a typical target will be the master file containing standing data. Another target will be the collection of transaction files, which before, during or after processing can be accessed and altered.

Computer crime has already spawned its own jargon with terms such as 'piggy backing', 'salami technique', 'data diddling', 'logic bombing' and 'Trojan horsing'. 'Piggy backing' means illicitly tapping across a data line in communication with an authorised user and then using the said user's identification to gain access to the computer. Cheap microprocessors enable simple devices to be made to separate and distinguish between several signals transmitted down a single line.

The 'salami technique' would now be the name given to the second example above where small amounts from many accounts were shaved off, transferred and accumulated in a special account. The classic means of doing so is replacing the rounding-off utility which averages out the slight inaccuracies by a salami software utility. 'Data diddling' is straightforward changing of certain data items with other items. 'Logic bombing' is the insertion of hidden routines, which are triggered by certain events or combination of events and which cause programs and data to be corrupted or overwritten. Experienced computer criminals use logic bombs to get the computer to destroy all records of their existence or activities if any inquiry is made. In addition logic bombs are inserted in some standard software packages by the vendor to stop a particular package from being used when a further licence fee is due. These can sometimes be accidentally triggered by the user with the necessary skills who attempts to get the program to execute faster by making modifications to the hardware. 'Trojan horsing' means giving instructions to the computer to obtain unauthorised information. Naturally much of the information concerning computer crime is not for publication.

According to a recent report by the FBI, computer-related crimes are growing at the rate of 400 per cent per year. It is difficult to charge computer crime because the statutes in force are not suited to framing charges and it is important that a circumstantial web of evidence from sources other than the computer be made to focus on the accused if there is to be any real chance of successful prosecution.

Lawyers faced with charging or defending computer-related crimes should refer to some of the books and articles cited in Appendix C. Undoubtedly computer-related crime will soon be one of the most important areas of legal activity.

References:

(1) Parker, D. *et al. Computer Abuse*. Stanford Research Institute, USA, 1979.

(2) Norman, A. R. D. 'Computer frauds — are they a manageable risk?' *Accountancy* October 1976.

APPENDIX C
Further Reading

British Computer Society. *Control and Audit of Minicomputer Systems*. Heyden, 1981.

Carey D. *The Computer: How it Works*. Ladybird Books.

Hansen P. B. *Operating System Principles*. Prentice Hall, 1973.

Institute of Internal Auditors. *Recommended Codes and Practices for the Audit of Data Processing Activities*.

Large P. *The Micro Revolution*. Fontana Paperbacks, 1980.

Longworth G. *Standards in Programming*, NCC Publications, 1981.

Mellor G. and Rickaby J. G. *Data Processing Documentation Standards*. NCC Publications, 1977.

National Computing Centre. *Where Next for Computer Security?* NCC Publications, 1976.

Nora S. and Minc A. *The Computerization of Society*. MIT Press, 1980.

Report of the Committee on Data Protection. HMSO Cmnd 7341, December 1978.

INDEX